TALES
FROM A
TECHNOCRATIC
CITY

EINDHOVEN
FOOTNOTES.

ONOMATOPEE
161

Tales from a Technocratic City:
Eindhoven Footnotes.

The editing of the book will use the various synonyms and definitions of Tales to separate the content. I decided to do this as it gives me some distance from relating specifically to technology as the project was as much about building a narrative and network as it was about *Actual Real Critique*. Using these terms also allows the research and writing to distance itself from the scientific, and allows for a wider, more imaginative interpretation of results and actions. Tales are open to different readings and cooption, yet ultimately stand the test of time as they pass down action through the immateriality of voice and memory.

The cover design references the graphic
work done by Callum Dean for the original
Eindhoven Footnote zines.

The Story

Josh Plough

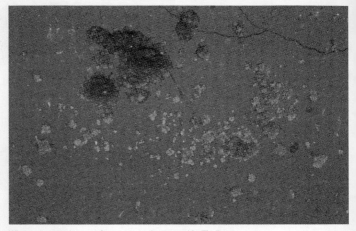

When you see clumps of manure on the ground in Eindhoven you can be 99.9% that a police horse has been there. These traces are the physical and often overlooked manifestation of power in the city. While on Stratumseind, the longest bar street in the Netherlands, we see a shift in perspective. It's a perfect example of invisible policing, with six smart cameras, 64 microphones (per acoustic camera) and 22 lampposts with mood influencing lighting, nestled above our heads conveniently out of sight.

*These numbers were correct when the original zine was published.
There are probably more now.

The city of Eindhoven, in the south of the Netherlands, is terrified of its own insignificance. It has rebranded itself eight times over just as many years.[1] But this terror isn't felt on the streets, in the markets or at the gym. It's felt in the PR department of the city council. It's an imagined inferiority complex when a post-rural then post-industrial village, then town, then city tries to show its *value* and relevance on an (inter)national scale. It seems it's no longer enough, or maybe even viable, for a city to exist with and for its residents. It has to exist for investors, developers, entrepreneurs, companies, influencers, technologists, researchers, academics, brands...the list goes on and on.[2] It's because of this executive decision to see the city as an entrepreneur that Eindhoven has been pushing its latest branding strategy: The Smart City. It feels like a cynical move, to invite surveillance technologies and their subsequent companies with their vested interests onto its streets just so it can become a *leading city of the 21st century*.[3] In label only.

Eindhoven Footnotes, a year-long (re)search project, is the driving force behind this publication. Its main focus was on the presence of technology on the city's streets, the ethics associated with mass surveillance, laws, concerned citizens and the complicity and pretty much blind ignorance of the city council to the ramifications all of these things. Over the course of the year five zines were produced.[4] The contents of which contained research, writing, and projects related to the companies and technologies found on the streets of Eindhoven. Departing from the usual formula of similar projects with their data visualisations, highly designed projects and speculative thinking, Eindhoven Footnotes was grounded in the belief that the building of mutual networks of trust and criticality could bring about *Actual Real Critique*. It was when Footnotes hosted the becoming.network that *ARC* was discussed. The idea being that criticism alone is not enough, as we have to actively propose and build viable alternatives. Just making the 'invisible visible' seems almost twee now.

It was because of funding from Cultuur Eindhoven and the Creative Industries Fund NL that the whole project could happen.

Partnerships were forged with the local technical university, design academy and heritage house meaning that a mix of students, specialists and members of the general public could meet and discuss technology and citizenship. This subsequently called into question the efficacy of design research. How radical, really, is all of this critical research when more often than not it ends up as a passive hyperlinked PDF, an object sat in a gallery or a **book**?

But it was not just the financial support that allowed this project its freedom to explore. Onomatopee trusted it enough to let it focus on the less tangible implications and 'results' of its research; like when it was mentioned by council members or brought up at public meetings. It meant that a curator, instead of just exhibiting critical works, could position themselves as a conduit through which research finds its way into corporate offices, the Gementee, and onto the desks of bureaucrats and hopefully, brushing up against local and national law. Wishful thinking it could be. But staging these scenarios and meetings is the first step towards something.

Distancing itself from the project slightly, this publication takes its editorial direction from the tale: *a fictitious or true story, especially one that is imaginatively recounted.* By creating a framework around storytelling the open-ended nature of design and art research, together with the intangible nature of network building, is best contained and expressed. The report, the saga, the parable, the account, the fable, the allegory; all of them allow the subjects of technology, citizenship and the city to be explored with imagination. By labelling them as such the research undertaken also distances itself from the scientific field. A plasticity is introduced, a more lyrical way of discussing the challenges cities and their technologies face. Another reason for referring to all these projects through the lens of the raconteur is to flatten and enmesh the research undertaken. To get the mind going so it makes associations between the seemingly different approaches of design research and investigative journalism.

The Report sets the scene. An interview concerning the state of privacy and internet freedom in the Netherlands with Lotte Houwing, policy advisor and researcher at Bits of Freedom.[5] From there we can work our way through essays, design projects and collages. For *The Saga*, Bas Grutjes (local Eindhovenaar, activist and writer) investigates the murky presence of technology in the city and the Netherlands; finding data breaches, links between research done at the local technical university, racist language and the tracking down of migrants, to name just a few. It truly is a Saga, one that shows our connected world to be as corrupt and closed as it ever was; despite what the branding and corporations extoll: *openness, transparency and autonomy*.

For *The Tale*, writer and researcher Sjamme van de Noort explores the idea of 'truth-spots' as means of building more open and transparent systems of knowledge production in the city. Touching on the dodgy links between EU funded smart city initiatives and China's autocratic regime[6], the essay makes a call for providing the public with the lab coats and instruments they need to *actual*-ly participate in the city's Living Labs project, instead of merely functioning as their lab rats.

A selection of design projects feature throughout the book too, acting as counterpoints and alternative plot devises. They appear under the title of *Allegory* and can reveal different ways to interpret the written research they're suspended within and next to. Projects like *Materialising Data* or *Lichelligence* may not be immediately recognisable as critical technology projects, but when you spend time with them you can wonder and imagine what the connections are between crumpled and dirty paper, the symbiosis of urban lichens and systems of surveillance.

In *The Account*, designer Helen Milne exposes us to the tensions between a smart city, residency and protest. How has it come to be that a city hoovering up data to improve its services is so blind to the housing crisis that it faces? Its PR departments scream INNOVATION at you through its websites and social media channels. Yet it's so inflexible that it can't seem to tackle the most basic of rights. The whole palaver lays bare the dissonance between PR dreams, sensory digital culture and the lived reality of a city.

Networks can be established but they have to be maintained. And hopefully through storytelling these narratives can keep on resonating after the project has finished. This is the belief focused on in *The Parable*, where the emphasis is on squeezing the debate out of studios, exhibitions spaces and conferences. If we're to find a future where we tackle all the negative aspects of connected technologies and the narrow lenses they watch us through, then we have to keep telling these stories, over and over again. Including more voices as we go, while embellishing the stories as they travel between people, cities and contexts.

Finally, this is not an anti-Eindhoven book nor is it simply *about* Eindhoven. The politics and issues that are entangled in this southern Dutch city are the same ones that knot all smart cities together from China to Germany. Eindhoven has though made admirable steps towards opening up the debate surrounding technology and citizenship. But we need to continually and forcefully ask if this isn't just smoke and mirrors. The supporters of its local football team (PSV) organise anti-surveillance protests with chants of "We are not Criminals, We are Football Fans"; the city hall is refreshingly approachable; its local politicians can be open and willing; and there are literally hundreds of creatives, academics and citizen journalists researching and acting in the city. But for things to change all these people need to meet.

All welcome, all free.

1
The City of Light, Eindhoven City of Sports, Eindhoven Leading in Technology, Eindhoven the City of Knowledge, The City as a Laboratory, Eindhoven the City of Design, Eindhoven Creative City, Eindhoven Brainport of the Netherlands.

2
It's worth noting that Eindhoven, when compared to other post-industrial cities in the Netherlands and Europe, is doing well economically and in terms of "livability"

3
https://www.eindhoven365.nl/en

4
Titled: Criticism in the City, Not Knowing the City of Knowledge, Weird Archeology Faux-Ethnography, How a City Listens, Letters from the ISE Technology Think Tank.

5
Bits of Freedom is the leading digital rights organisation in the Netherlands, focusing on privacy and freedom of communication online. Working at the cutting edge of technology and law, Bits of Freedom strives to influence legislation and self-regulation, and empower citizens and users by advancing the awareness, use, and development of freedom-enhancing technologies.
Donate here: https://www.bitsoffreedom.nl/jarig/

6
Even more pertinent now given the hyper-draconian reaction to the Hong Kong protests and the Covid-19 virus.

Tracing Identities was an archeological expedition into Demer, one of the main shopping streets in Eindhoven. The research was conducted without an objective of what to look for or discover. It was an investigation that tried to detect the invisible, underlying structures of power and influence shaping an innocuous shopping street.

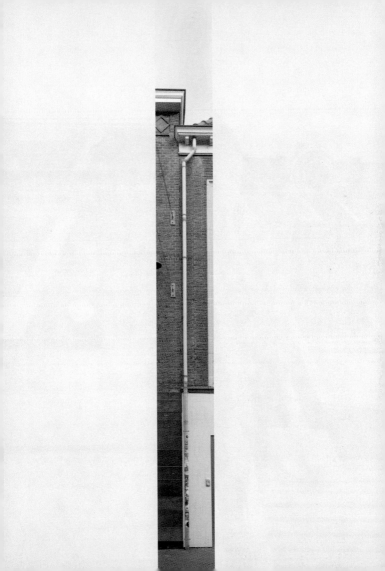

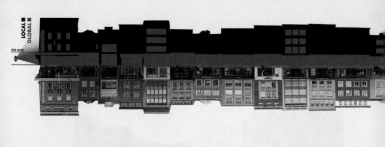

The panorama above shows the street view of Demer, Eindhoven—the western side—and a schematic map of the same view divided into space occupied by global (green) and local identity (black). Note: although it appears as if a majority of the area is still *local*, walking the street leaves a very different impression, because on the ground floor there is hardly anything that isn't *global*. Only by looking up above eye level does one see larger parts of the local architecture.

The Report

Lotte Houwing
Bits of Freedom

BoF: Bits of Freedom is a not-for-profit, an NGO, working on internet freedom with a focus on privacy and freedom of communication online. We started twenty years ago when it was a niche thing, and it was kind of clear what the internet was and what it wasn't. But now the internet is everywhere, so it's harder to make a clear boundary between what our field of work is and what it isn't. I personally work on privacy and the relationship between the state and the civilian. So more related to state surveillance, while my colleagues work more on things like freedom of communication and problems with platforms. So in the end we're a diverse team. Currently I'm working mostly on privacy in relation to the police and the secret services, we're also expanding that because relationships are more and more fuzzy. There are commercial companies who have big financial interests in the marketing of smart cities where predictive policing is implemented. So then you can ask the question who is pushing the project, is it still the police or is it more the financial interests coming from the surveillance industry? And how does this threaten our privacy? Also it's not just the police or the secret services anymore who are surveilling people, it's also the tax services or organisations monitoring people who are living on benefits. So there are other services from the government as well who are getting more and more invasive powers.

J: It reminds me of the relationships between insurance companies and fitness trackers, where they give you lower premiums if they quantify your life and measure your behaviour every minute of every day.

BoF: Yeah everything gets connected, you know. And that's why years ago it was easier to say, "Ok, I'm working on this subject, and this and this are the boundaries of it". That's harder to do because it's turning into one big thing.

J: And so in view of everything mentioned and your position with privacy and police, the secret service, citizens and also this creep of commercial interests, how do you see the Netherlands and its state of health in terms of surveillance? Is it doing well, is it failing? Who has the power?

BoF: Who has the power is a good question. I think it's pretty much under pressure at the moment. It's not even that people are actively giving power away, willingly or at least consciously. I think it's going step by step and a lot of people are not seeing it yet. For example the FaceApp app was a big hit, but not everybody, well most people, aren't reading the conditions under which you send your face to companies like that. So people use it and then it's a hit and people have the hangover: "oh whoah, I never realised that I gave my face away and it can be used to train technologies to develop facial recognition systems. Which we might then see on our streets meaning I can't walk through my city anonymously anymore. I don't want this!" So I think we're working against ourselves because there's not enough consciousness to see what we're doing and what the consequences are of the choices we make about our data and the use of technology.

You see it in apps, you see it on Stratumseind [Eindhoven], where it's meant to be one big experiment and with all good intentions, but in the end if you add everything up that's happening there: it scares me. I published an opinion piece that can be used as a comparison, it's about the situation in America with the Ring Doorbells [Amazon product]. The police have cooperation agreements with Ring asking them to make posts about the company, and offering free products in return. There's this agreement between the company and the police, where the police benefit from free access to a portal where citizens who have the doorbell are connected. So it's easier for the police to access the pictures from the civilian's cameras, that's their benefit. And Ring is promoted by the police, that's their benefit. And in the end people end up hanging cameras everywhere because the police and the company are working together and giving people the feeling that they're unsafe, so they have to put up cameras, which makes them more unsafe because their right to privacy is invaded, and there is no proof of a drop in criminality because of the presence of cameras. So this really weird dynamic of financial benefits and safety interests are teaming up, and we don't even know where it's going because I don't see what the real benefits are of filling a city with cameras.

J: No, I think it always benefits just a few people. Someone from a university in the UK came to talk to me about the project and was asking, "How can we change this?" I thought that as long as the knowledge or our way of understanding is obscured, the less we'll be able to critique and defend our rights. One of the fallacies of the smart city of Eindhoven is that they say "We're open and transparent and we give your data back to you: we're giving you data sovereignty." Which is kind of bullshit because after interviewing and talking to people you realise that no one knows how to process this stuff. So they're harvesting for the sake of harvesting, potentially monetising it (with things like the Citybeacons), but then they say "but you can have your data and you have the possibility to make money from it". But I have no idea and don't understand how to deal with raw data.

BoF: Yeah, and you still don't have a choice. They legitimise their projects by saying, "you can also benefit", but maybe you're not interested in the financial gains of harvesting this data and you'd prefer your right to privacy, then you're just fucked.

J: Completely, and what I find interesting is that after doing workshops with members of the public the reactions, more often or not, are "but this would never happen here"; when I talk about China or I talk about what happens in the US. "We're too democratic for that to happen". Do you think that's a misguided public opinion, that "it's never going to happened here"?

BoF: I think that there is more happening in the Netherlands than you might think at first sight. But it is less in your face as in for example China. But in the end a lot of data is gathered about citizens in the Netherlands, and systems get more connected to each other, which is also like a net that is tightened, but it is less visible than hanging biometric surveillance tech in the public space.

J: I read a piece about the smart city of Utrecht and the language surrounding the debate was feverish. The guy behind the initiative in Utrecht was saying that he would rather have these sensors on every street corner than soldiers. So here you have this really bombastic and violent language used to legitimise the existence of these things.

BoF: If you give people a false choice, either we're gonna do this or something worse. Then suddenly your first option seems quite reasonable. I think we should more often ask ourselves the question: do we want this at all? What are the benefits it's bringing when you compare it to the situation when we didn't have this technology? Who is feeling safer now in Stratumseind [Eindhoven's party centre], and for what reasons? What problem are we solving with the implementation of this technology? And what will be the societal effects?

J: And can you see a place for the art and design in this debate?

BoF: The fact that we had the referendum, and the changes that are made now might not be much, but still the fact that we could have a referendum and there was this message that the majority of the voters said no. It was because the message got through and I especially think this is a spot where art could mean a lot. To just engage people with the subject and to maybe explain in a different way what's happening, because for us we work in a legal framework. I mean I'm a legal researcher, so for me this is the way to talk about it and you try to make it as accessible as possible and to translate it to normal human language. But I think art can make a different translation, and makes it possible to engage other people to talk more about these acts, surveillance and what it means to a society. What would an alternative society look like, if we skip surveillance? Would it be that problematic, because now we've chosen a path to make use of these technologies. If we skip it, where would we end up? This kind of thought experiment would be really great to have in an artistic manner.

J: So, do you have a positive outlook in terms of our relationship with technology?

BoF: People shouldn't look at technology as the one bright solution. For a lot of different problems there are a lot of different solutions, and sometimes this is going to be technology and sometimes it's not. So we should look for the best solution and not just the shiniest one; or where some companies can make the most profit. And I also don't like it when it comes out of a feeling of fear, with surveillance that's mostly the case. I like technology in general, it's just something that humans can create to enhance their possibilities, allowing us to do things we weren't able to do before; but we shouldn't forget about ethics.

What if?

27

What if?

Results of workshops conducted by
Pete Ho Ching Fung and Eindhoven
Footnotes with students from the
International School Eindhoven

what if Instagram is the only platform that gives us
the news?

↳ NO MORE NEWS channels on TV
↳ NO MORE NEWSPAPERS
↳ NO MORE NEWS Accounts (official) on other
   platforms.
~~people need to foll~~

SO

→ when having an Instagram, you
   get mandatory news accounts to follow.

→ Volunteers are available for people
   that need help to use Instagram.

→ FREE WiFi open for everyone
   (just like EHV city)
          dh

(→ Instagram is not only for news thou)

→ Newspapers, news channels, .. all need
   to notify their audience that
   they will need to use Insta for news.

adv:
* more time for educational TV
  shows/carton;
* reduce paper waste
* you get both side of the story
* censure → no

disadv
→ only way to read the news
  (you don't have a choice)
→ Men needs to get Instagram
  or know how to use it;

Ways to advertise/ solve the problem:

limit the time
for the users to
go online per day. ←

bring Istagram ←
into the
real world.
(physical)

What:
became the
of inte
between

↓

<u>Problems:</u>

people will have no
social ~~school~~ skills.

↗

Istagram
only way
by
humans?

→   friends will only be
made through internet

↘ Istagram will be the
main control of the
community.

— <u>Who makes it?</u>:

— DIVISION OF LABOR = PEOPLE NOWA[...]

NOT EVE[...]

— DOES IT HAVE OWNERS?

WHO MAINTAINS IT?

— SPECIALIZED AUTOSALOONS / OWNER

— IT IS USED AND BOUGHT BY A CERTAIN TYPE OF PEOPLE.

Wh

ARE SPECIALIZED ON SPECIFIC TOPICS.

↯

E SMALLEST PIECE OF TECHNOLOGY CAN BE MADE BY 1 P.

has control over it?

____ of course ... But: with the development
technology, digital becomes more and more
with the "physical" world. This makes it Hackable.

••• who codes the cars?

ELF DRIVING CAR:
LD IT MAKE MY SAME DECISIONS?

("
_ DM would'nt be private anymore, since anyone can know who's texting who.

Los would prevent lie and cheat, since you can get caught easily!

> Instag become private pe

("
what if email on not everyone's and our in

Everyone would have accent to everyone else's data, So you would know what your followers research, do....

uld
ately

▷ .We could see whoever
checks our profs.

⌐ We would hacr, who
is interested in us. But
everyone else who is following
you could also know.

could get an
ation , with all,
am data, information

↳ We would
Know, How many
people have research
our name.

— — what if all teslas ··· be

would it be good? SUSTAINABLE?

- what if Elon musk, buy sure technology electric self charge cor.

- what if the company TOSCA suddenly shut

Wh

- What if tesla made tanks to.

27/05/2019

- what if the products had coloured indicating their ecosustainability?

- What if we ~~distributed~~ advertised (and tasted) partly, with a ~~% or resources in general~~ re were explained out loud?

- People needed to produce every thing of buggy?

d affordable for everyone?

someone, would come up with an

en. all of

if ...

on their back (GREEN/YELLOW/RED)

at the end of it, the consumption of electricity, water,
for the production of the products consumed

needed by themselves, without the possibility

WHAT if

You don't use techn...
But technology uses...

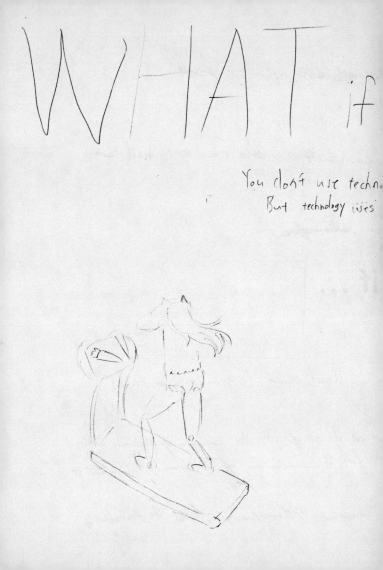

The Saga

Bas Grutjes

The Daleks are among us

This is no Dr. Who fan fiction.
It is about the city...spying on you.

Shedding light on the deep darkness around City-beacons and smart cities in general

Abstract
You are systematically spied upon when walking down my street. The municipality sells your private data including your exact where-abouts, to a commercial enterprise, without you ever even know-ing it. Why? In return, the municipality gets to occasionally show a silly statement on some digital billboard, telling passers-by for instance that it's almost Christmas again. It's for free, for the municipality, as you foot the bill unknowingly.

This is the story of the Citybeacon, and the Living Lab, but also of smart cities worldwide.

It's a story about what's happening, and why it is bloody dangerous. In this story I will get angry. I'll make some bold claims. But I will also prove those claims.

I'll touch on some big subjects beyond privacy & freedom. I'll show that our government protecting our civil rights is just a joke when we're talking about your and my data. I'll argue that democracy is seriously harmed by opaque public-private partnerships such as the "triple helix" organisations, and that your autonomy as a per-son is fundamentally threatened by smart cities themselves.

I will also talk about climate crisis, rising authoritarianism, the remaining sources of hope, and ways to resist. I'll try to answer the question if resistance against the smart city is futile or not.

Resistance is at any rate necessary, and I think you will largely agree with me on that after you've read this essay. I will by the way also show that the city council of Eindhoven (Netherlands) was lied to by its own administration, that the fast embrace of smart cameras and other sensors by our country was at least partially motivated by corruption, and that the faces and maybe biometrics of tens of thousands of citizens have been leaked in a massive data breach. And this is quite harmless compared to some other stuff I'll share.

There's even a little fable involved, so please, do start reading.

If you've got any of my nerdiness, you have heard about the Daleks. An alien race of cyborgs who seek to completely control and ultimately destroy the universe. Well, today they don't just populate the great science fiction series of Doctor Who: they are here, in our streets, at this moment. Yet exactly nobody is paying them any mind, let alone posing any opposition.

Their invasion started in Eindhoven. Of course, they renamed themselves, as these villains are clearly not as stupid as they seem in Doctor Who. "Citybeacons" is what they call themselves nowadays, and they are a totalitarian nightmare.

Citybeacons are high-tech, steel columns featuring big screens that show video advertisements. There's also a smaller, interactive screen attached to it that gives you *incredibly* vital information about the city centre ("you are now near some stores").

You find Citybeacons in the streets of Eindhoven, but they are rapidly spreading: Amsterdam Arena wants them, they are in the streets of Indonesia, they have a foothold in Silicon Valley, and Saudi Arabia is very interested. Giant corporations like Intel and Microsoft generate free publicity for them.

They promise you free Wi-Fi, and can be counted on to annoy you with their looping video commercials.

But is that all they do?

I wish it were.

While many among us associate the word "beacon" with light, hope, democracy, even freedom, the Citybeacon is everything except those:

It is a spy column.

43

Rant

One morning, some four years ago, I came back from a visit to the city centre feeling concerned. I had seen the Citybeacons for the first time, and I didn't like them. It wasn't just the annoying flashy ads that tried to take my attention away from my friends and the tiny bits of beauty that can still be found in our inner cities. It wasn't the crass stupidity of the information that it offered. No, I had a nagging feeling there was more to it. So once back home, I tried to find out what that more might be.

This proved quite hard. Although the municipality claims to be proud about Citybeacons, and the companies behind them yell things like "Smart city platforms!" and "Omni-channel reach!" nobody is actually very clear about what they do exactly.
The more I researched, the more my heart was filled with rage. This is what I wrote later that day (well, actually, in the middle of the night after hours of work):

"OK... so I must have missed something. Some commercial venture has gotten permission from the city of Eindhoven to place 25 "Citybeacons" in our streets. I had seen one of these ugly things before, but I hoped it might be something temporary.
Alas...

Citybeacons are not just intrusive outdoor advertising tools. They serve as a spying tool.
These things are filled with cameras, count passers-by, sniff your phone, and they even try to track your social media, according to Eindhoven municipality announcements.
To make matters worse, concrete information about what specific data the Citybeacon collects is completely missing. Does it record the MAC (identification number) of your telephone? Probably, but we can't be sure. Does it track your movements, logging every place you've ever been within their range? I guess so, as the municipality has proudly announced that it is used for crowd con-

trol. How exactly does it view your social media, and what data is stored from your phone?

And, no small matter, who can actually access all that data and what do they do with it? Unclear, folks, disturbingly unclear.

As a concerned citizen, I want to know if someone is spying on me. But apparently the municipality didn't see a need to tell anyone. Only if you search high and low, scanning hundreds of media reports, advertisements, business-websites and annual reports, and putting in quite some hours of work, will you get a glimpse at the larger story.

The Citybeacon itself doesn't give any info about its capacities. The website that goes with it is just a bland advertisement. But it isn't hard to guess. This is a commercial company, functioning in cooperation with "public order services", that is to say, probably with the municipality, police, environmental service, and possibly commercial anti-terrorist organisations. We already have some experience with that on Living Lab Stratumseind.

Living Lab Stratumseind is an ongoing experiment in Eindhoven, in which citizens are the unconsenting guinea pigs. Stratumseind is a street filled with pubs and also sensors, including smart video cameras, MAC sniffers, and street lights with 64 microphones per lamppost[281], which track every movement of every visitor, matching the data with data harvested from social media, GSM tracking and other sources.
Living Lab is not only about monitoring and harvesting massive amounts of data, though: the goal is to influence people's behaviour, 'nudge' them, through the use of lights that change colours and intensity, artificial smells, and other means. This experiment has been running since 2012.
A similar project is running at Living Lab Strijp S, the city district where Philips once produced consumer goods in big factories. Philips moved out, the factories stood empty for a while, and were then filled and gentrified with creative industry. The city looks upon the district as an experimental playground with great

revenues, important for the economy, technological innovation and their city marketing.

When you enter the district, a city traffic sign says: "If you can see this, we're looking at you." The district is filled with sensors, cameras, and even 'sound-cameras'.

There are more living labs in the making. Vitality Living Lab[1] invested 5 million euros to harvest data from the bodies of runners and the public at the local Marathon, without asking them for permission. There are plans for a living lab at the Victoriapark.[2] Eckart-Vaartbroek, a neighbourhood "filled mostly with social housing in need of extensive renovation"[3] is another, together with "Brainport Smart District".[4] In 2016, a large 15-year contract was granted to build a citywide 'smart lighting grid'.[5] Bee Smart City explicitly says this about the project: "the Citybeacon is just the tip of the iceberg"...[3]

Eindhoven, fifth largest city of the Netherlands, is very involved in city marketing, as it seems to see life as a constant struggle between major cities of the world, competing for economic superiority. Eindhoven presents itself as a "Brainport", a smart city of innovation and design, one which could play a crucial role in the world with its focus on big data, sensors, and security.

Their focus is less on people themselves, or supporting their living a good life, unfortunately.

Commercial companies exist to earn money, and Citybeacons are owned by one. Your data will therefore probably be resold. And, given the monumental lack of foresight of the municipality of Eindhoven (as far as the privacy of its citizens is concerned) you can count on the fact that there is little data that is *NOT* stolen from you and re-sold.

I would really love to be proven wrong on this score.

Right wing law-and-order parties are known for dismissing privacy as irrelevant, and for declaring the open market sacred. But Eindhoven has, and has had, a largely centrist/left-wing city administration. In spite of its leftist tendencies, however, "public-private partnerships" are the order of the day in Eindhoven. In other words: every conceivable part of life is marketed, enabling the business community to lay its hands on almost all the private information of its citizens.

Looking for fresh ideas and sources of money, the municipal government has completely tied itself up with commerce, in opaque and often questionable arrangements. Citizens have no idea that anything in particular is happening, and although the municipality knows that *something* is happening, they have no idea what, or how big it is.

The most typical example of this surfaced in a conversation I had some time ago with a privacy officer employed at a multinational, who wished to stay anonymous out of fear of losing her job. Her company collaborated with the municipality of Eindhoven on the excessive prying and spying going on at Stratumseind, where every passer-by has been closely monitored for years. She told me that the multinational she works with had to ask the municipality to please share *less* private information about individual citizens with them, as this is absolutely forbidden by law...

This is a world turned upside-down, one in which a data-hungry multinational shows more concern for your privacy than the government that is supposed to protect you from invasive corporate greed.

There are two things about the Citybeacon that could be useful to citizens, at least in theory. It has a sniffer that measures air quality—OK, you might not be able to use it directly, but it's useful, and the data it generates do have an open format.

Secondly: it has a Wi-Fi hot-spot. But how many people still need Wi-Fi these days, and how many are willing to log in again at each post? Also: think of the word 'Wi-Fi Server' as 'Wi-Fi Sniffer' – sharing free Wi-Fi is a great way to spy on your phone; finding out where you come from, where you go, what gets your attention so you stand still for a moment, what will probably influence you, and how to squeeze more money out of you.

> **Quotey quotes!**
> ***Principles for the Digital City***[7] *(as introduced by the city of Eindhoven, also embraced by Amsterdam)*
> *"Residents know what equipment has been installed in 'their environment', can exercise an influence on that equipment, and can make use of it. (...)*
> *The data about the resident belongs to the resident; the resident is owner and decides what happens with that data."*

No one asked for these Daleks. Nobody hoped for yet more intrusive commercials, flashing in your face on big screens. Nobody hoped for an unprecedented merging of government and the business community, which as a result can monitor every step you take and sell the collected data to the highest bidder.

You might logically assume the municipality makes a huge profit from this project, as it must surely be lucrative to sell your citizens' personal data, along with your own principles as a government. There must be a huge reward, that they would grant CityBeacon BV permission to fill the city with those Daleks. After all, even for a simple signboard above his shop window, a shopkeeper pays sky-high sufferance tax.

Dream on. They have granted Citybeacon BV *free* permission. The "payout"? The municipality itself may occasionally place some information on the screens. "Hi folks. Next week it's Design Week. Hurrah." "Eindhoven: the best shops in town." (Actually, I made up these slogans. The real slogans are even worse. They are devised by Eindhoven365, a city marketing organisation that tries to take gentrification to a new level, and manages to take actual pride in that.)

This is how much worth our local government places on your privacy: Businesses are given your data for free and are allowed to spam you with annoying ads, as long as the city may spam you with some city marketing bullshit, too.

Fuck the sale of government and society, fuck the control and surveillance frenzy, fuck the distrust of citizens, fuck people who think they can reduce your life to some digits, and fuck city marketing. Above all, fuck 'smart' cities!"

Breathe

...Was this a moderate text? Is it *nice* to declare that the municipality demonstrates "a monumental lack of foresight"?

No.

But maybe the very existence of Citybeacons means going beyond nice, softly spoken words, even if these things do have the microphones to hear you, however softly you choose to speak.

Two and a half years later, apart from my text being shared a lot on social media, with the municipality and some city councillors tagged, nothing much has happened. No answers came to any of the questions I posed. Nobody else bothered to write negatively about Citybeacons. The city council only asked the municipality once what Citybeacons actually do, and the answer they got was factually incorrect.

So now it's time to put some effort into the search, to find out more about these spying columns.

What data do they harvest? What sensors are inside? Is there an effective governmental control mechanism? (TLDR: NO.)

What does this say about smart cities in general?

Is resistance possible, or utterly futile?

Dear reader, a long read follows.

The Search for Information

Even before I began my research my state of alarm was already high, as I had recognised the Citybeacons to be a major intrusion of the privacy of all those who happened to use the streets and innocently stroll past these Daleks. But my research only made my worries grow.

The trouble is, there's barely any publicly available information about the things. If you type 'Citybeacon' into the local government website, you get zilch. On citybeacon.info[8] there's no info, just advertising. When you search deeper, you get some hits on websites linked to the government, but no hard info. The open data portal of Eindhoven[9] says the machines are "provided with information and apps, which contribute to bringing relevant city information for residents, visitors and entrepreneurs in the city. Sensor data is also generated from the Citybeacons. For the time being, these are the air quality data."

No word about what the other data is that can be generated from passers-by. Living Lab Stratumseind–the triple helix project that is spying on people walking along that street – acknowledges the "data harvesting" by Citybeacons[10] but doesn't specify anything further.

All I can do is read what is written in the media about it. And that proves quite revealing in itself. For instance, the Citybeacons don't just have cameras, they have microphones too.

Citybeacons BV Director Bart Knipscheer claims in an interview[11] that his machines will not collect any information that can be traced back to an individual. This is a claim that is repeated again and again: data are "anonymized." But the same interview ends with the journalist asking: "And what about combating criminality and public nuisance? Knipscheer: "We can place cameras and sound sensors".
That anonymization seems painfully short-lived...

Almost all information about the Citybeacons follows this pattern. First, we are lead to believe that the Citybeacon is harmless, and with great self-assurance some official insists your privacy is *ab-so-lute-ly* assured. Then in the next sentence or shortly after, it turns out this is untrue, or at the very least uncertain.

According to the municipality, all sensors except the air pollution sensor are shut down, because of the GDPR, or as it is called in the Netherlands: AVG [12]. This privacy law forbids the collecting of personal data without active consent. It came into effect in 2016, but was unenforced before May 2018.

Yet two months before, with the AVG already in place for two years, Eindhoven247 wrote proudly [13] they had activated three security cameras. And that they are developing a "Smart City Dashboard" that links data harvested by the Citybeacons with several other data streams, one of them being Vodafone's GSM data. Eindhoven247 happily announces they will be able to track where you came from, despite the AVG intended to protect you and every citizen from exactly this scenario. And that is not all: individual movements are remembered. Eindhoven247 will know if you "were here before, and if you came by car or train. Information that is very relevant for marketeers!"

Anonymisation, my ass.

Anonymisation

In 2016 journalists from NDR [14] (German state television) proved they could legally buy the anonymised browser records of several million Germans, and track back these records to real people. For instance, they discovered a judge visiting S&M porn websites, they found many people (and their names and addresses) looking for drugs, etc. The journalists didn't break any law during their investigation. By the way: German privacy laws are actually much more strict than Dutch laws are.

Who owns you?

Staf Depla [15] (former *wethouder*, responsible for the placement of the Citybeacons, still in office when he said this): "If NAM gets the Dutch natural gas out of the ground, it has to pay for it. But if we as a municipality want to re-use our own data, do we have to pay for it? I don't think that's okay." That is why he wants the government to own the data that are harvested by sensors in the city.

What is a wethouder?
The structure of Dutch municipalities is organised similarly to European countries. You could see the mayor as the prime minister of a city. The local ministers are called "wethouders," responsible for initiating policies and managing the municipality. They have to answer to the local parliament, known as the 'gemeenteraad' or city council. While being wethouder is a full time job, the members of gemeenteraad only work part-time.
I'll use the Dutch word 'wethouder' in this text, as no exact translation for it exists in English.

There's just one small problematic detail: wethouder Depla talks about the municipality re-using "our own data". But it's not the government's data. It is your data, your life. This is one robber complaining about another robber: "They shouldn't steal the stuff I want to steal!"
The wethouder doesn't legally own any of it. It's the individual citizen's data. The discussion shouldn't even be occurring between government and business, as it should be a well-informed decision made by the people who ARE in fact the data, a decision that simply needs to be followed up by the forces that come begging for your data. The government is one of those forces, actively distrusting citizens and seeking to control them, while it should be protecting them, putting individual autonomy, human dignity and rights first.

According to Eindhoven 247, [16] the municipal organisation that installed the columns together with CityBeacon BV:
"User data is also generated from the Citybeacons. From air qual-

ity, traffic information and social media data to usable data such as visitor numbers...Citybeacon provides security, communication and information functionalities... Observation cameras (crowd control & camera surveillance)".

In plain English, Citybeacons are in fact spying bots. The Citybeacon films everybody around the advertising column, with the cameras hidden from your view. That is how Citybeacons could film your reaction to a commercial...

Comparison: The Dutch railway scandal

Not long ago there was a lot of commotion about cameras at Dutch train stations that did exactly that. Hidden smart cameras recorded every face looking towards their outdoor advertising, following your eyes and algorithmically interpreting your facial expression. Valuable information for advertisers, for sure. The NS, the national train network, was well paid for the cameras on their grounds. But when people learned about the secretly recorded videos, the public outrage was great enough for the NS to end it immediately [17].

It wasn't just outrage that made the NS think again, it was also the fear of lawsuits.
According to researchers at eLaw (Center for Law and Digital Technology), observing people with hidden cameras is a breach of law [18], and the mighty Dutch supervisory organ Autoriteit Persoonsgegevens basically agrees [19]: you need permission from the people themselves when you point cameras at them, and you need it beforehand.

In Eindhoven however, nobody seems to know or care about the possibilities of cameras inside an advertising column. Eindhoven247 and CityBeacon BV might have found the legal loophole they were openly searching for, to enable an evasive manoeuvre around the privacy laws, but if they did, they never told the public. Hush is the operative word.

Spying tools

Although Citybeacons have been in place for four years already, there still isn't much we know for sure about them. There's no warning posted for passers-by, and indeed that wouldn't do much good anyway, since your only option is to avoid the inner city altogether if you don't want to be monitored. Opting out is otherwise impossible.

The columns contain Wi-Fi trackers. And I already guessed so when I wrote the rant this article starts with, four years ago, but now we know for sure[20]: They can record the unique MAC address of your phone when you pass by with either your Wi-Fi or Bluetooth activated.

Given the acknowledged monitoring of social media[21], a good question is whether the Wi-Fi trackers also contain a Wi-Fi packet sniffer[22], which is a tool to read every mail and see any web page that a nearby phone or laptop is viewing using Wi-Fi, provided the person isn't using encryption like SSL. I am not saying that Citybeacons use packet sniffers – I just don't know if they do, or how they would otherwise 'monitor social media'.

Citybeacons do contain cameras and microphones, as well as an NFC-, RFID- and an iBeacon chip. Two of the cameras are "audience tracking cameras" which can differentiate men from women, make educated guesses about your age, and even record your mood by identifying the emotion behind facial expressions. This is all admitted by Richard Ponjee[20], manager at Eindhoven247. Openly and with pride.

He does contradict himself though. In March 2018 he tells podcast Rush Talk[23] that some of the cameras inside Citybeacons have facial recognition, but that the only people that can use them are the police. However, in October 2018 Ponjee tells Eindhovens Dagblad that Citybeacons can't take selfies any more because of laws concerning facial recognition.[24] If that is so, does this mean the police took selfies up until October? Or could the first claim be untrue, and did Ponjee's enterprise enable people to take selfies, so it could harvest biometric data about them?

The only thing we know for certain is that the two claims by Ponjee can't be right at the same time.

Should you not want to be filmed by Citybeacons, and should you feel you ought to be able to hide your face, well, sorry, you might wish that but it won't do you much good, it seems. Intel announced in 2017[25] they'll install Intel® RealSense™ cameras[26] into Citybeacons. These cameras project an infrared pattern onto their surroundings, so they can build a 3D image and apply facial recognition[27]. They can follow your hand, finger and face, and decide what you look like, and what you're looking at. Even in the dark. Once that data is linked to social media profiles, they will automatically know the names of most people passing by.

Now for some good news
According to the municipality most sensors have been shut down by the new privacy law, the GDPR (or AVG as it's called in the Netherlands).

Alas, as we'll see there are quite a few question marks around this claim.

Other sensors in Eindhoven Smart City
Sorama builds smart microphones for Living Lab Strijp S and Living Lab Stratumseind. The so-called "sound-cameras" don't actually contain any cameras, but build an image on the basis of what their microphones hear. They can even hear and track bicycles. In their own commercial on YouTube[28], they show proudly how a perfectly normal guy strolls on the side walk, then starts to run for a bit, and just that automatically triggers an alarm on the phones of the neighbourhood watch (buurtpreventieteam) saying: "aggression in sector xxx, please respond".
"Long live the free and open democratic society," right? Just don't repeat that quote too loudly, lest you set off their alarms...

Who is behind the Citybeacons?

Intel isn't the only multinational interested in partnering with City-beacons and providing free commercials for them[29]. Microsoft is doing the same[30]. The first iteration of the Citybeacon was designed in New York in 2013, by a company that's acquired by Verizon since then[282]. This is in no way a small, local initiative. But there are many Dutch players, too.

The two companies behind Citybeacons in Eindhoven are City-Beacon BV and Eindhoven247 BV. This last one is a privatised part of the municipality, derived from the Eindhoven Marketing Foundation and it's the sister organisation of Stichting Eind-hoven365 foundation. While Stichting Eindhoven365 was involved in placing the Citybeacons and using their data for city market-ing, Eindhoven247 BV is responsible for the exploitation of Out of Home Media such as the video advertisements on Citybea-cons.

According to the Chamber of Commerce[31], Citybeacons BV is based in Rotterdam, on the exact same address (a luxurious but small villa) as a company called "Shiny Investments BV".
How is that for a trustworthy name?

The cameras and software in Citybeacons are supplied and oper-ated by its partner ViNotion[32], which in turn is also a close part-ner of DITSS, owner[33] of all AI cameras (also by ViNotion[34]) and microphones on Living Lab Stratumseind.

DITSS

DITSS seems innocent and trustworthy enough: the Dutch Insti-tute for Technology, Safety & Security is listed as a non-profit foundation, with a supervisory board[35] that consists of several mayors, a police official, and someone from the public prosecu-tor's office. Looking closer, we get a different picture though. DITSS describes itself[36] as a 'management organization" func-tioning as an "independent broker", which means that what is done by DITSS, is really done by their partners, with DITSS as the innocuous-seeming umbrella organisation providing a layer of opacity.

1, 2, 3, 4, 5, 6 Helix

DITSS was set up when Rob van Gijzel was mayor of Eindhoven. Van Gijzel was a big promoter of innovation and the idea of solving social problems with "triple helix" organisations. This is management speak for hybrid organisations, in which government, industry, and universities work together. It is an organisational model that has become very popular in the world of smart cities.

In practice, this approach leads to a hidden form of privatisation, in which the government outsources their core tasks (such as providing security) to commercial enterprises, sharing massive amounts of data about citizens in the process. The critique that triple helix is in fact locking out citizens while deciding on their fate, led to more Orwellian "Newspeak". The term triple helix was mostly replaced with quadruple helix, and even multi helix. The first term is management speak for involving citizens, and the second for involving nature itself, though this is mostly unadulterated bullshit. For instance, the municipality of Eindhoven claims in its strategic review of digitization of the city[37], that it's essential to involve citizens in every decision. This is even "more important than our principles" (...) By page four it names the *city council* as a sufficient and acceptable option for collaborating with citizens, as the politicians are formally intended to represent them and their interests. You could call this a democratic loophole to NOT have to actually work with citizens.

(How we could go into business together with *nature* as a partner in multi helix organisations is yet to be discovered...)

Quotey Quote
"For what concerns the citizens, Public Value is not demonstrated clearly."
This seems to be the most important sentence of Eduard Gualandi's (otherwise mostly positive) master thesis[38] about the financial sustainability of Living Lab Stratumseind.

The umbrella that blocks your view

Back to DITSS. Interestingly, we can't see who their partners are. We are only introduced to some of them, the ones that look good or at least inoffensive: cities like Eindhoven, universities (TU/e and Tilburg University), the well-known research organisation TNO.

If we really dig around, we do find more partners. For instance, VCS Observation[39], which is one of the partners with whom DITSS started Living Lab on Stratumseind. VCS's core business is video surveillance, including facial recognition[40].

Another partner is SIVV. At first glance, this seems to be yet another non-profit foundation... In this case, the umbrella becomes almost invisible. SIVV advertises with the possibility for entrepreneurs and the self-employed to become "participants", and as they advertise:[41] "all SIVV participants are full DITSS partners." All you have to do[42] is give them 500 euros and 5% of whatever money you make under the umbrella of SIVV (3% if you get assignments through them, but handle them under your own name). Bonus: you even get free business cards for that princely sum (for real!)

Can any idiot join? Well, it seems you need to work in something connected to security. Defence is named as one of the eight fields in which SIVV operates; clearly a nice opportunity for weapon dealers who have fallen upon hard times.

Am I exaggerating now? No, sorry, wish I were.

Tracking down refugees

After the end of the Cold War, the military-industrial complex had a problem: defence budgets were cut everywhere, and not nearly enough people were murdered in wars to keep shareholders happy about the bullet sales figures. Lucky for them, 9/11 happened. And just when the fear of terrorism began to subside in the following years, a new problem was invented. Fears around the "problem" of refugees were stoked (that is to say, not the many, pressing problems faced by refugees, but rather pitting citizens against the people themselves.) Soon, this was followed by stoking fears of all migration, with the exception for the migration of the wealthy and white, of course. We are mid-process of a large-scale militarisation of national borders,[43] which is being expanded to include more and more of our cities, as well. Weapons factories aren't limited to producing just weapons any more. Their product lines have diversified greatly; they now also produce drones, heat sensors, smart cameras, and many other tools used to automate the manhunt for refugees. If you survive their bullets, let's see if you can survive their borders. It remains a win-win for the arms dealers.[44]

And, surprise surprise, DITSS, TU/e and ViNotion reappear once more. Happily working together[45] in PASSAnT, a smart camera system that automatically "tracks down refugees"[46] as they put it, in the refugee *hotbeds* of Moerdijk and Oostende. In Cursor, the TU/e magazine, the people that are rounded up with the help of this "intelligent system", are called "gelukszoekers"[47], an explicitly racist, derogatory slur for migrants.

Is this the 'social responsibility' and 'privacy first' that Tinus Kanters, public face of Living Lab Stratumseind, keeps making power-points and presentations[48] about? (There[48] seem[49] to[50] be[51] endless[52] numbers[53] of[54] them[55].)

DITSS owns[33] the cameras and microphones on Living Lab Stratumseind. But how can anyone assume these cameras to be 100% privacy friendly, when the owner is not just a non-profit founda-

59

tion, but also a multitude of businesses that share an important side business: making money by hunting down refugees?
Who makes sure that cameras in Stratumseind and Citybeacons are not also tracking down refugees, given that the companies responsible for those are also making money doing precisely that?

You could say the government will make sure. But if my research proves anything, it's that the municipality and the businesses behind Citybeacons and Living Lab are each telling a very different story, effectively taking away credibility from both narratives. Today, public control is simply not trustworthy, as I'll show.

> **Quotey Quote**
> The Hague Centre for Strategic Studies[56] names DITSS, the organisation involved in Living Lab Stratumseind, as a possible partner for **commercial defence- and contra-terrorism activities from *outer space***[57], through *observation by satellite*. It's the observation of buildings, people, everybody and everything, all the time. The Hague Centre names it as an enormous "**economic potential**", especially for **"the public security sector"**. The sky is no longer the limit; space is.

Privacy is secured!

We don't hear much from Citybeacons about privacy. But we sure do hear a lot about it from Living Lab.

Main Characters: Tinus Kanters
Tinus Kanters' star rose back in the eighties and nineties, when he was one of the leading organisers of rock festival Dynamo Open Air. At its peak year the festival was attended by 118.000 paying visitors, after which the gates were knocked down and even more people streamed in for free. Somehow Kanters became known as one of the countries leading crowd-control experts[58] after that.
Kanters is a friendly guy. He looks and talks like an old-school

rock-n-roller of the hippy-kind. The type that was educated as a social worker in the seventies–and indeed, so he was. It's an image carefully maintained: rather than in his free time, he wears festival T-shirts during presentations. He's the absolute opposite of what you expect when you think of a typical project-manager, working with multinationals and government in a project that spies on citizens. And that is probably exactly why Kanters is the ideal public face for that.

Kanters is project-manager of Living Lab Stratumseind, and he's seconded by the municipality to DITSS in part-time.

"Living Labs project leader has the University of Tilburg on his side, to carry out checks to make sure none of the experiments harm citizens privacy."[59] Project-manager Tinus Kanters has been telling people for years now that Living Lab is *good* for privacy. He did change his tune a tiny bit lately, asking the public to be more aware of data harvesting. But he also complains that he has so much data to offer, even demographic data (obtained how, exactly, Tinus?) that "isn't even used by anyone yet!"[60] Still, he claims privacy in Living Lab is secured.

His arguments:
1. *The people behind Living Lab consider privacy as very important.*
   This claim is deeply weakened by their various secondary activities, such as the building of facial recognition tools.
2. *Everything is anonymised.*
   As we already know, anonymisation is mostly a farce, since individual users can be tracked back on the basis of 'anonymized' data. Journalists proved[61] that they could do that without much effort, on a major scale.
3. *'We collaborate closely with the University of Tilburg, where there's even someone getting her doctorate researching privacy aspects of the Living Lab!'*
   We haven't heard from Living Lab about that last research much lately, certainly not since Maša Galič indeed published her PhD[62], concluding that even with anonymised data as it is generated by Living Lab: "this

mode of power can still affect individuals, particularly by limiting their possibilities of action (including via nudging) and potentially **limiting their autonomy**. (...)
[If the project expands throughout the city] broader **privacy risks concerning society and democracy are imminent**."

Living Lab Stratumseind simply failed the checks that Kanters was boasting about.
The only thing we can be sure of is that the government's protection of citizens against power hungry data-grabbers is an almost complete failure, as I will demonstrate.

History is what's happening

Back in the nineteen thirties, the Netherlands had an advanced administration system. The civil registry didn't just note your name and address, but also your religion and ethnicity.
When the Nazi's invaded, they had little trouble finding and deporting Jews. They just walked into the Dutch population register to look up where they lived.
It was not just the registry. It was also the many Dutch policemen that collaborated, and there were many other causes too. But the fact is that, while even half of the 500.000 Jews that lived in Germany by 1933 were able to flee and survive, only 24% of the Dutch Jews survived. 63)

There was resistance, nonetheless. The Dutch resistance bombed the Amsterdam population registry, to prevent the Nazi's to use it for the Holocaust. The attack failed partially: only 15% of the records were burned. Most resistance fighters involved, were arrested and killed. 64) Still, their act of heroism saved many: 15% of the 80.000 Amsterdam Jews 65) is still 12.000 people.

It's very depressing to realise what would happen if a new group of Nazi's would come to power now. We could try to bomb a data centre, but it would be useless, as data is kept in a multitude of places.

The law under surveillance

Some think laws are meant to bore other people, not them. Well, ignoring laws certainly led to a massive leak of fun in this case, but not the kind that you might expect or hope for.

What does the law actually say about the limits of Citybeacons and similar sensors aimed at people in European cities?
Not as much as it should. The European Commission says new rules to restrict the use of AI and of facial recognition [66] by businesses and government should be made as soon as possible. There is an important law that already applies, however, and that is the EU General Data Protection Regulation, also known as AVG.

Almost all data harvested by Citybeacons are considered personal data, whether collected by the Wi-Fi tracker that records the unique MAC number of your phone when you walk by, or the microphones or cameras that track your movements through the inner city. The same goes for most sensors, cameras, and microphones at Living Lab Stratumseind, the ones at Living Lab Strijp S and probably for the Smart City Dashboard as well, which, among other things, collects and processes data from social media.

Both Ponjee (of Eindhoven247, Citybeacons) and Kanters (of DITSS, Living Lab Stratumseind) seem to think that when personal data is anonymised, it's allowed.
But this is simply not true.

From the Autoriteit Persoonsgegevens [67], the Dutch data protection authority:
If a company immediately makes camera images of passers-by in a public place anonymous, is that still a form of processing personal data?

> "Yes, even when images are immediately anonymised, and for instance only the number of passers-by is recorded, this is still a processing of personal data.
> Processing personal data is not just collecting, but also

deleting or changing personal data. This means the AVG must be applied, and you need a lawful basis to be allowed to do so."

Of the six possible bases in law, only one applies to cameras and other sensors in advertising billboards in public spaces, like the Citybeacons. That one legal basis is that *everyone filmed, recorded or whose MAC address is taken, must have given consent beforehand.*

Even in cases when consent is given, people have the right to know how these data are processed, by whom, and what is done to keep the data safe. They also have the right to look into the data, and to be forgotten (= removed from the system).

But Citybeacons.info doesn't even have a privacy page. Nothing notifies passers-by that the Citybeacons have sensors aimed at them, and that they may be filmed. Yes, some streets leading to where the Citybeacons stand do have signs warning that there is police video surveillance present. However this is not true for all streets, even though it is a legal requirement for the police cameras to do so. Worse: None of these signs warn for anything else, other than the police cameras. There is no mention of audience tracking cameras, nor for any of the multiple commercial sensors within the Citybeacons.

The AVG embodies a hard informational obligation, and this obligation is clearly not being met. Foundations like DITSS and companies like Eindhoven247 BV and CityBeacon BV, who own cameras in Living Lab or Citybeacons, are breaking the law, day and night, even if they were to be using old-fashioned, non-smart cameras. (And we already know their cameras are far from old-fashioned.)

Why are biometric data far more dangerous than just your picture?

To collect and process biometrical data, such as fingerprints, facial recognition, walking behaviour (gait), iris scans or *anything*

64

that can be used to identify a body, the requirements are much higher than what I mentioned above. This makes sense, especially for facial recognition, as this is one of the few techniques to identify people at a distance without them even noticing they are being filmed. Once your facial features are in the database, you can be recognised everywhere in the future, often even when you put on a hat and grow a beard.

Bits of Freedom (organisation "for privacy and communication freedom") showed how this works in a shocking experiment. Their researcher Paula Hooyman did a test with the public live stream of a webcam in the centre of Amsterdam, and facial recognition. Using the free trial period of Amazon Rekognition they could automatically recognise a person just walking by the main square. [68]

On the right you see the biometrics that Amazon Rekognition extracts from the photo on the left. Image by Bits of Freedom [68], [CC BY-NC-SA 4.0] [69]

After the biometrical extraction of the first photo, this second image, 20×26 pixels only, made in the street from a distance by a public webcam on the Dam square, was enough for the facial recognition software to recognise researcher Paula Hooyman of Bits of Freedom. [CC BY-NC-SA 4.0] [69]

Amazon Rekognition is AI software anyone can buy: it costs only one dollar per 1,000 processed images; cheaper if you process more than a million images a month. Basically Bits of Freedom proved that any stalker (and any oppressive regime anywhere in the world) can monitor his victim without even leaving his home, just using publicly available sources.

But actually, this goes far beyond being able to go anywhere without strangers knowing what you do, and with whom. Facial recognition AI is increasingly able to know very personal details about our inner being, and can tell things about us from a distance, that some of us don't even want our family and loved ones to know. Scientists applied facial recognition AI to simple snapshots of white people on a dating site, and were able to automatically predict if a person was gay[70] from a photograph, with 81% accuracy for men and 74% for women. This was already accomplished in 2017; the developments have been extraordinary since then. You can only imagine what would happen if Singapore, Egypt, Morocco or one of the 73 countries[71] in the world where homosexuality is forbidden, would decide to scan citizens' passport photos, and automatically track down and round up all people that the algorithms claim are gay. China shows us that this is not a matter of *if*, but simply of *when*. (More on China to come, I'm afraid). The same goes for many other features that AI can extract from pictures and other biometrics, even if you as a human might not spot it at all. We are closer to the realisation of the movie Minority Report than we've ever been.

The Minority Report is a story by Philip K. Dick that was made into a movie by Steven Spielberg. It's about a bio-mechanical computer containing genetically altered mutants, that is used to predict murders. The Pre-crime Division of the police arrests everyone labelled as a future murderer by the computer system. Without any trial those people, who have not broken any law or done anything wrong, are put into permanent artificial sleep.

When he wrote the story, Dick was mostly interested in the existence or absence of free will. But the other theme of the story has proven to be as or even more important. While he might not have expected predictive policing to ever become real, the Netherlands is now the first country in the world that claims to predict crime nationwide[72]. The Dutch police force uses a data-mining algorithm that's called CAS, Criminality Anticipation System, which tries to predict in what neighbourhood crimes will be committed. "Crimes" must be interpreted broadly in the case of CAS: the minister names the prediction of "nuisance by adolescents" as one of its goals.[73)] Another one is "schennis van de eerbaarheid", which can be public masturbation, but also for instance showing your buttocks to a policeman, or topless sunbathing.

There have been incidents: A totally innocent woman driving home from work was cornered on the highway by the police, after "the system" took her for a drugs runner. On Living Lab Stratumseind, police rushed in with lights flashing and sirens wailing when CityPulse, the predictive system built by DITSS and Atos, took dancers for rioters.[74)]

More artificial intelligence (AI) systems for predictive policing are being built around the globe. By 2017, Chicago predictive identification software[75)] had already put 400.000 citizens on a black list because it expects them to commit a crime in the nearby future.[76)] There is a lot of criticism of predictive policing: it is not accurate and leads to the fallacy of reification and to racial profiling[77)]. The ACLU states[78)] that predictive policing is actually better at predicting police practices than it is in predicting crimes. Amnesty International calls predictive policing the "complete subversion ... of notions of innocence and guilt."[79)] American human rights organisations[80)] and scientists have called for a ban on any form of automated decision systems, and for transparency when they are still used. A government task force is now researching ethics involved.[72)]

In the Netherlands though, almost nobody seems to care. There are no laws in place about AI, automated decision-making, or predictions, and the Dutch police force can experiment with AI and predictive policing as they wish. Minister Sander Dekker #1) refuses to disclose the algorithms used.[81)] The only law that says something closely related (art. 11 Wpg[82)]) basically says the police can automatically compare any data-sets they want.[83)] The minister of Justice and Safety announced that he wants to review the Wpg to make this even easier.[84)]

Shockingly enough, he names the pro-AI lobby organisation Nederlandse AI Coalitie (Dutch AI Coalition) as a triple helix organisation that must *ensure "ethic standards"* when AI is used by the police. Amongst the partners that form this lobby club, we find some strong links with Living Lab Stratumseind (TU/e, Brainport Eindhoven (DITSS) and The Hague Security Delta[85]) but also companies like Booking.com. (you can rent yourself some privacy there huh, and even a 'privaat' as the Flemish call a toilet, so they must be privacy experts!)

Showing dictatorships how to do it

In the (according to Human Rights Watch[86] 'stifling authoritarian') Republic of Singapore, Minority Report is named as a positive goal worth pursuing for predictive policing.[87] A team from the Singapore police force, that uses robotics and AI for predictive policing, came to the Netherlands last year for inspiration, and were shown around Living Lab Stratumseind by DITSS.[88]

Singapore is democratic in name, but opposition is pestered. Surveillance is massive, even all medical files are part of the monitoring of the population for 'terrorism' or 'self-radicalisation'. The country has one of the world's highest execution rates relative to its population. Singapore knows no privacy rights, has no freedom of expression, and demonstrations or indeed *any* gathering of more than five people without prior consent from the police are penalised, e.g. fines or even caning.[289]

The visit to Living Lab Stratumseind "was a real eye-opener" to the Singapore cops, says DITSS. The organisation behind Stratumseind Living Lab was invited for a counter visit, and is happy to come to Singapore soon. DITSS is eager to learn more about the way in which the authoritarian regime "operates the police units in the field, using robotics for surveillance."[88]

Even if there's no predictive policing involved, facial recognition is still a very bad idea.

Ironically, the fact that facial recognition also has a high failure rate makes it even scarier. The South Welsh police use facial recognition to identify wanted criminals in crowds. Their system is an abject failure: 92% (more than 2.000 people) were wrongly identified as criminals, while only 8% of the hits were right.[89] Still, the South Welsh police force continues to defend (and use) the system. The city of London wants to copy it, claiming that the success rate in their own tests was 70%. An independent review found a very different factor though: only 14%, with 86% false positives.[90)]

Facial recognition systems have an even higher error rate with people of colour, which makes it from the outset an ethnically discriminatory tool, even when not deliberate.

When does the law permit biometrics?

The processing of biometrics and other 'special categories of personal data', as is the case when you collect walking patterns or apply facial recognition, is *forbidden by default by Dutch law*. There are six possible exceptions to that general ban.[91)] Of those, organisations like DITSS or Eindhoven247 can process biometrics only when:

1. The subject has explicitly given permission for one or more clearly specified purposes, and is able to use the service even when he or she refuses biometrics.
2. When processing is a necessity for authentication or security purposes. *But only* if there is no other, less invasive way to achieve that goal.

Counting people and tracking their movements with Citybeacons or Living Lab Stratumseind / Strijp S is not a necessity, nor is processing biometrics the only way to do so. People do not give permission for it, nor is it possible to enter the streets without being processed. In short: there is simply and clearly no way in which private entities like CityBeacon BV, Eindhoven247, or DITSS are permitted to track people or use cameras on them.

Citybeacons process biometrics. It is likely the only way several Citybeacon columns can track movements of people through the inner city: a person must be identified with a tracking number to let the next beacon know it should pick up the trail when that person is getting out of range of the first beacon. The same goes for the cameras at Stratumseind.

Eindhoven247 said it can also tell how many visitors are returning visitors. [13)] This means they don't just track a person during one session, be it by MAC number, gait or by facial recognition, but their system is able to remember and recognise that same person even half a year later.

Eindhoven247 knows it is processing biometrics. Manager Ponjee said in a podcast that some Citybeacons have facial recognition cameras.[23] He also told the local newspaper[24] Citybeacons stopped offering selfies because it was against the law, "because of facial recognition". It's important to note that this is the only time when Citybeacons or any of the associated parties acknowledged that they use facial recognition at all. The municipality seems completely oblivious to this and the many implications that go with it.

They also process different kinds of special categories of personal data, since they acknowledge their cameras can differentiate between men and women, ages and even moods.[20] Combined, these data provide an enormous amount of information about a person, which is exactly why it's illegal to do so without that person's expressed permission.

Breaking
We caught Eindhoven247 / Citybeacons on a massive data breach of photos and probably biometrics, that continues to this day.

Wethouder Staf Depla was interviewed about sensors and the smart city in July 2017 by the FD newspaper[93]. He showed the journalist around town, and they stopped to take a selfie at a Citybeacon, with a photo-filter of a silly hat. Depla then discovered on the spot that his picture was automatically shared on social media. "Did this thing just send my photo to Facebook? No way! That's absolutely not allowed, we must do something about it!"
According to FD the wethouder did indeed take action: soon after, pictures were not placed on Facebook without permission any more.

However, Rutger Schimmel just discovered that literally thousands of pictures were also shared on Flickr. I Investigated. The 72.600 high-resolution pictures contain about 108.000 recognisable faces. Quite a lot of those belonging to people in the background, passing by without realising that their picture is being taken.

All of the photos are still there. Most are posted under a Creative Commons license, meaning that any person or company can take your photo from Flickr and use it as they wish, even modifying it or using it for commercial purposes, as long as they give credit to "Eindhoven City Selfies".

In the examples printed below, I covered up the eyes and used a low-resolution to make people unrecognisable.
On Flickr they are still shown full face, and in much higher resolution.

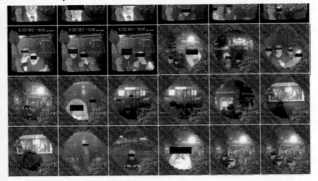

(Photos by Eindhoven City Selfies, [CC BY-SA 2.0][94], edited by Bas Grutjes)

Photos of children and drunk people

Quite a few of the people featured are pulling strange faces for fun or seem to be drunk, as the Citybeacons are near a lot of pubs. Quite a few of the photos could create unwanted attention and trouble if for instance an employer, or potential employer, were to see them. Many people pictured are clearly small children or seem underage. Many were posted long after Staf Depla made

71

sure that the photos were not posted on Facebook any more: the last few were published in May 2018.

We made a formal complaint to the Autoriteit Persoonsgegevens, and hope that the photos will actually be pulled offline by the time you read this. Whether the pictures are still online or not, in the case of a data breach like this, a substantial fine would be justified. Breaches of the AVG can be punished with a **fine of 20 million euros**, or (if that's higher) 4% of the organisation's worldwide revenue.

The Autoriteit is unfortunately very understaffed, and given that even wethouder Depla hasn't been able to fully shut this down, this massive infringement of privacy may still continue as you read this.

Even once the photos are taken offline, the privacy infringement probably continues, given that Richard Ponjee (Eindhoven247 BV) confessed to the newspaper Eindhovens Dagblad that the City-beacons used facial recognition[24] when taking the selfies. We already saw that extracting biometrics is much more than just a picture on a website: in facial recognition software, feature extraction is used to obtain your biometric identification data. With these data, machines can identify you at a distance, without you even knowing it.

How is it possible that this happened without people knowing? And what happened to the biometric data? Who has the data now? Are the people in the pictures recognised everywhere they go? If so, then by whom? Are those biometrics out in the open, deliberately, for everyone to grab, just as the photos themselves are?

The power of politicians

A salient detail: It's not just thousands of citizens whose selfies are exposed. I wondered about the selfie of wethouder Staf Depla, the one he was rightfully furious about when the Citybea-con posted it on Facebook without his consent...would it be on Flickr? It was quite a lot of work, I looked at more then 20.000 strangers, but yes, there he was. And it's still there now as we print this. Even the wethouder of Eindhoven proves to be incapable of getting his privacy treated with respect by CityBeacon BV and Eindhoven247 BV.

Addendum: new data breach

Although we wrote above that the photo's were removed from Facebook, during the correction round for this text we found out that they were... posted again. And apparently someone is eager to put names to the anonymous faces.

During Kings Day, massive festivities are organised in Eindhoven by Eindhoven Is King, an organisation directed[95] by Eindhoven365 and co-organised by Eindhoven247.[96] Eindhoven Is King published hundreds of Citybeacon selfies[97] on Facebook in 2018. **They even ask the public to tag** the (mostly drunk) **people with their names**. In 2019 a repost follows with the same question; apparently it's the sort of information they want enough to keep asking for.[98]

Failing governmental control

Triple helix organisations lead to what the Dutch call "a butcher inspecting his own meat"; the government can't be a fully independent inspector of an organisation in which it is itself involved. Beyond a general lack of knowledge, this can help explain why the monitoring of those doing the monitoring is so incredibly lacking.

73

Eva de Bruijn, city councillor for GroenLinks, is clearly worried about the growing amount of sensors and the privacy threat they represent. When I spoke with her (before discovering the biometrical data breach), she expressed measured optimism about DEDA[99], which is a model meant to assist data analysts, project managers and policy makers in recognising ethical issues. "But that's just a first step."

When I check the model afterwards, her comment seems an understatement, to put it generously. The model is nothing more than a poster listing some questions to consider. It leaves it up to data harvesters to handle the identified ethical issues as they see fit. As it is set up, the poster could even be used to find excuses or cover stories, to push through questionable practices despite privacy violations. It's not really clear this is actually a first step. Neither the municipality nor the developers of DEDA have made any mention about continuing development, or at least I couldn't find it. The takeaway message seems to be that they think this is enough.

City council was misinformed about Citybeacons

Eva de Bruijn wants more, though, certainly where information is concerned: "GroenLinks believes that the information position of both citizens and councillors must be greatly improved with regard to the digitization of services, sensors in the streets, and the smart city in general," she tells me.

De Bruijn and two city councillors from other parties expressed concern about this, formally asking the Mayor and Executive Board for details on what exact data are collected by the Citybeacons. In July 2018, the wethouder answered that cameras are turned off[100]. "Only the environmental sensor [for air pollution] is collecting data. (...) No other data is collected."

That seems misleading, or at the very least **misinforming the city council**, given that Eindhoven247 announced three months earlier [101] they had **turned on** three cameras.
In their annual statement at the end of the year Eindhoven247

again acknowledges performing crowd control on King's Day[32)] with ViNotion, using audience tracking cameras that can also detect "deviant behaviour", according to the builders. [103)]

Eindhoven247 goes on to write that there was a lot interest for their test by the municipality... but how is it that the mayor and wethoud-ers were very interested to hear how big masses of partying people were tracked with cameras in Citybeacons, and then immediately after that forgot all about it? Why did they, only three months later, tell the city council that the cameras were not activated?

This was not a one-time occurrence. In an interview with Josh Plough and Rutger Schimmel, Arthur van de Poll (CEO CityBeacon BV) acknowledged that King's Day wasn't the only day on which the Citybeacons cameras were switched on, despite the AVG. According to Van de Poll this also happened with Glow, another mass event, one that lasts for a week in November. So the munic-ipality must have asked CityBeacon BV to switch on the cameras and tracking *after* it led the city council to believe the cameras are always off.
The city council was clearly misinformed, or in plain English: lied to.

More vagueness

Plough and Schimmel asked Van de Poll why the data that were harvested are not on the open data portal, so everybody can see what's harvested. According to Van de Poll, there's no need to share anything, because it's just a test. Schimmel, looking back on the conversation, tells me: "That's clearly nonsense. They just use the cameras whenever they want, it's not a test or an exper-iment, but simply the deployment of cameras and tracking devices for crowd control."
Also, Richard Ponjee told the Eindhovens Dagblad about ending the selfie-function[24)] of Citybeacons because of facial recognition on October 18th 2018. Why then did the wethouder tell the city-council that all the cameras and sensors were off three months earlier, while facial recognition cameras were turned on at that time?

Quoty Quote
Plough remembers: *"Arthur van de Poll (Citybeacons BV) said to us: 'The Citybeacon is the Rolls Royce of data harvesting.'"*
Schimmel: *"With some options turned off, some of the time. He said: 'It's a Rolls Royce, disguised as an Audi. Still good, but less luxurious...'"*

There are more examples of contradictory claims by the companies behind Citybeacons and the municipality. Wethouder Depla said that all data must be owned by the city[93]. In the "principles of the digital city"[7)] the municipality of Eindhoven decided something else: "The data about the resident belongs to the resident; the resident is owner and decides what happens with that data." But according to Eindhoven 247 BV (regarding Citybeacons): "all data remain the property of Eindhoven247."[95)] Oh?

Also, already in 2015, the city ruled that "data collected in public spaces are always a public asset. (..) The municipality always knows which data are collected in public spaces." [105)]
Unfortunately, that is clearly not the case at all. Reviewing the answers to questions posed by council members, the wethouders don't even understand the difference between audience tracking cameras, facial recognition, police surveillance and audience counters, and there is no record of them even mentioning the NFC, RFID & iBeacon chip that the Citybeacons have. For that matter, no government website names them, either.

According to the wethouder[100)], the actual list of sensors and data is shared at the open data portal of the Eindhoven municipality. But the portal only names a few[106)], certainly not all. It vaguely states that the Citybeacons combine "among other information, signs, antennas and advertising in one column. (...) sensor data is also generated".
If you are to check the analysis tab on the data portal, you'll find that the surveillance cameras have an "on/off" option, but the accompanying diagram only indicates an "off" and an "n/a" where you would expect an "on". Both are indicated. This means we

can't see if the cameras are on or off, as it will result in the same status at the portal.

Evidently fewer sensors are named than the beacons contain, and two sensors have incomprehensible names as well as indeterminable purposes (RD_X & RD_Y).

Furthermore, the sensors of Living Lab Stratumseind are nowhere to be found on the city's open data portal.

Up until very recently another website[33] at least told us what sensors are used at Stratumseind and who the owners were. But that site was in test phase for the few years of its existence, and it contained only some of the sensors. It didn't share the data itself, although those are supposed to be "open". The website was still online when I started to write this article; now it's gone. Even when it was still online, the website already seemed outdated as links to the open data portal didn't work. It has not been replaced with something else, as far as I could find.

> **Quoty Quote**
> An interview by Innovation Origins [107] with Richard Ponjee (Eindhoven247) ends like this:
> *"It is typical for the municipality and Eindhoven247 that Citybeacons are already here and can do utterly impossible things, while lawmakers are still busy building adequate policies. Municipality and Eindhoven247 want to be in the vanguard and experiment with new technology. They want to know the opportunities and risks."*
> The rationale for the existence of smart cities, their values or ethics are never seriously questioned in this process, it is simply assumed to be an unavoidable reality. As Ponjee says:
> You'd better be ready. *"We're moving towards a data-driven economy. And that data comes from sensors. Like those in the Citybeacons."*
>
> Whether you like it or not?

What will happen next?

I hope politicians will feel obliged to respond to the questions I pose in this essay.

Living Lab and Citybeacons will probably too. If they are smart, they will focus on one or two questions they have a nice answer to, and ignore the rest. I guess they will rather not talk too much about the data breaches or the illegal activities that I point out here. But they are in luck: I also note a lot of question marks with things I'm not sure about (hence the question marks).

For instance, I don't know how the data from social media are harvested. Maybe it's not a problem, the way they do it, or maybe it is. I'm sure some of my questions can be answered with very reassuring words. I'm also (very) sure that this is not the case with all questions that I pose, as I think I've made clear by now.

But just for the sake of argument, what if all my allegations prove to be wrong? What if the children in the photos all prove to be 18+ and all 100.000 people posted their photo on Flickr themselves? What if no personal data at all was processed by Citybeacons or Living Lab? And everything *is* really switched off, and it was just a bunch of hallucinating journalists that mistakenly wrote down wrong quotes?

What about Citybeacons with sensors that "are absolutely safe because they're switched off"?
Hmm. Why do we allow machines in our streets that contain sensors like that, if we're officially not planning to use them anyway? Can I bring a gun into the streets as long as I don't use it?
Do you think people will feel safer then too?

Seven more test-cases of governmental protection against invasions of privacy

1. Facial recognition

Meanwhile, the use of unregulated and in many instances unlawful facial recognition is dramatically increasing.

Without seeming to bother themselves with any questions of legality, the Dutch police are using it on asylum seekers and on Dutch suspects, keeping the records even if people are found to be entirely innocent. The system is named "Catch". There is no law that regulates this, but there are 1,3 million Dutch citizens [108] in the database now, and an additional 7 million (actual and former) foreigners[285], including all asylum seekers.

It is one of the many cases that begs demand for formal intervention from the Autoriteit Persoonsgegevens. But despite two budget increases, their funds remains far too limited; of the 20.000 complaints they received in 2018, just *seventeen* were processed with a view to enforcement. [109] That is less than 1/1000th.
Actually enforcing privacy is exactly this: 1/1000th of what it should be.

The general public doesn't seem to care all that much. Although the results are probably skewed–as the survey is done by Maurice de Hond*–with questions steered to favour right wing responses, with the (unjust) suggestion that only criminals will be followed, 52% of the respondents said that they think it's a good idea to place facial recognition cameras everywhere in the country [110].

2. Automatic number plate reading

Also in the news these days: The police illegally used automatic number plate reading cameras that are really meant to control pollution by traffic. [111] The Low Emission Zone-cameras are owned by the municipality of Amsterdam, but the police used them secretly, to follow suspects and automatically recognise convicts and cars. The municipality knew about it, for six years, but didn't tell their citizens. Now, at last, city hall acknowledged that the practice

79

was illegal, but Amsterdam is still doubting if they should consider it a data-breach, because, well, meh...

3. Ethnic profiling everyone on the highway

Roermond is openly profiling people, using a system with automatic plate recognition, cameras that count the number of people in a car, the colour and brand of it, and sensors that recognise the Sim-card and country of origin of your phone. Since 2018, the profiling system hands out points for the possibility that you are a shoplifter. The police gave this example [112] of what they consider a clear red flag: four people from Romania in a white car, driving towards Roermond's shopping outlet. They will probably be pulled aside by the law. According to the police this is very privacy friendly.

There are about 34.000 Romanian people living in the Netherlands. The police are actively profiling and following them, whether they do anything wrong or not. Also, you are now asking for trouble if you have three friends and a white car. Please don't drive near Roermond.

4. FSV: Ethnic profiling by tax authorities

The Dutch tax authorities have illegally stopped the childcare allowances of hundreds, and maybe thousands of innocent people. [113] Without any proof families were labelled fraudsters by machine algorithms, and then made to pay back thousands of euros they rightfully received. Although civil servants working at the tax collectors office protested [114] against the policy, high officials demanded they labelled people as fraudsters without proof, claiming that most would be guilty and the few that were not had to 'suffer with the rest'.

The result has been devastating: many people were caught in debt, some people were made homeless, there have been divorces, and one person has committed suicide.

The main difference between people labelled fraudsters and people labelled innocent seems to be ethnic profiling. Pieter Klein, one of the two journalists that got the truth out about FSV, estimates that two thirds of the victims of this illegal government programme have a second nationality.[277] Illegal registration of second nationalities, data-mining bulk data and searching for foreign sounding names, seems to be used to "find the fraudsters". The Autoriteit Persoonsgegevens is investigating [115], although the media now carefully avoid the word "racism".

Latest news: The tax office didn't just secretly mark hundreds or "maybe even thousands" of people as fraudsters, without any proof. No, it was at least 180.000 people that were automatically profiled as fraudsters by an algorithm ("Fraude Signalerings Voorziening", FSV), because of 'facts' like living in the same Postal Code area as some known fraudsters. Massive amounts of data about these 180.000 blacklisted people were collected, and kept indefinitely. They got extra tax audits that were extra tough, and were refused payment plans. Every one of them was treated as a fraudulent person, none of them were told, and because of that they weren't able to defend themselves against the accusation. This has been going on for almost twenty years. The automated system even used gossip as a reason to flag people as fraudster [116]

Autoriteit Persoonsgegevens finished their investigation and concluded the FSV to be discrimination and a serious violation of the law by government. [286] Parliament tries to investigate and put a stop to it for two years now, but is frustrated by misinformation from ministers time and time again. Ministers even admit that but refuse real transparency. [287]
New research by RTL Nieuws and Trouw suggests that this was not just the case with childcare allowance, but also with income tax. Another 150.000 citizens are labelled as fraudsters in this second system, without proof or trial. On the income tax-fraudster list are (amongst many others) parents that were unjustly labelled fraudster by FSV, and who are compensated for that now – but in the second illegal fraud database by the income tax division they are still known and treated as fraudsters anyway. [288] More Kafkaesque news will surely follow.

Although FSV was taken offline (a year after privacy officers already decided it was illegal—it was taken down only after upheaval in the media) this is not the end of merging databases,

81

automated decisions or AI in government. The development of new anti-fraud algorithms are already being announced. A new law proposal[278] for government services, commercial and non-commercial organisations to share data to combat fraud, crime and disturbing of the peace, basically legalises the illegal practise up till now.[279] It sets no legal boundary at all, and just makes it possible for the minister to set boundaries by Algemene Maatregel van Bestuur, that is: if he wants to, and bypassing parliament. The worst article in the concept proposal seems article 7a, which makes secrecy about collecting and sharing data possible.

Development of new algorithms and AI is not just about taxes. The minister of Justice and Safety just wrote to parliament: "Potentially, AI can be deployed with every police process in the future." [117]

5. SyRi

(Not to be confused with Siri by Apple, which creates immense privacy concerns as well [118].)

SyRi is another governmental Dutch AI system meant to track benefit fraud. It tries to link every database owned or accessible by government, and labels unsuspected citizens into risk profiles. When for instance data from a water company show that less water than usual is used at a certain address, this address is labelled a "wonder-address" by the algorithm, which is Newspeak for instigating extra surveillance by anti-fraud squads. Using less water or electricity than most people could mean that you are not living at the address that you told the government you are.

Every deviation of what the algorithm considers "normal" can lead to red flags for an address or person. Every governmental department or public service can look into these black lists. [119]

Risk profiling every civilian like this is an expression of the distrust of the state against its citizens. But while the state claims the right to absolute transparency of people's personal lives, the opposite is true for the state itself. The minister refuses to give any transparency about the algorithm used, and nobody is to know what's considered normal, what's a deviation, or why deviations should be considered a problem.

SyRi exists for five years now, and has been used in five cities, including Eindhoven. It has only been used on poor neighbourhoods, making this effectively a tool that discriminates people on income and ethnicity. Although the system must have invaded the privacy of hundreds of thousands of people during the past five years, not even one case of fraud was found. [120]

A coalition of NGOs like Privacy First and two columnists, has filed a lawsuit against SyRi for being in conflict with basic human rights. [121] The outcome of the court ruling is expected in 2020. (Update: Their resistance was successful, they won a landslide victory [122]. The judge opened the door to new initiatives like SyRi though, as long as they are slightly less invasive and a bit more transparent. No concrete norms were set for this.)

6. Sleepwet

In 2017 the Sleepwet [123] ('Dragnet Law', officially called WIV) passed through parliament. It allows Dutch Secret Services to eavesdrop on scores of their own citizens without having to provide individual justification or notification. They can legally hack computers everywhere in the world and plant false information on phones, even when owned by innocent people. The law permits them to massively collect the personal data of innocent citizens, and share that bulk data with foreign intelligence services without even checking what data are shared. [124]

There was a lot of protest against the law, and because of that even a referendum, in which a clear majority voted against the Sleepwet. But despite this protest of millions of people [125] against the Sleepwet, the law came into effect anyway, with only minor cosmetic changes [126].

The protests were fierce, as activists claimed (among other things) there are not nearly enough checks and balances to defend privacy and other citizens' rights, and the two institutions (TIB and CTIVD) that should defend those rights are toothless. Also, the TIB doesn't seem independent at all, as one of its three members is Ronald Prins, who is a former employee of the secret service AIVD, and another member is Jan Louis Burggraaf, who is also a member of the proto-fascist political party FvD [127]. As professor

Van Eijk of Information Law put it, the Sleepwet basically says to the Secret Service: "Everything is allowed".

After the law came into effect, the CTIVD did indeed basically conclude that civil rights are being violated. Despite almost "everything is allowed", it reported big risks of unlawful behaviour [128] by secret services in **December 2018**.

But that report didn't change anything. Matters didn't get better but got worse. CTIVD reported actual structural breaches of law [129] by Dutch secret services in **February 2019**. Even the TIB, with its former secret agent Prins, and Burggraaf, member of an extreme right political party, said in November 2018 that "too much is unlawful [130]". Then in **June 2019** CTIVD concluded that both the AIVD and MIVD were still not working in accordance with the law [131]. The AIVD's reaction was that they are very pleased with the report, as they made some progress...

October 2019, the CTIVD again concludes that both AIVD and MIVD are not upholding the law. [132] They are sharing data of innocent people in bulk with foreign secret services, without even knowing what data they share, as they didn't look into it themselves yet. The fun part is that they may do that, they are allowed to. The only thing they need to do, is ask the minister if they may. But she's not interested, and asked them to decide for themselves, although that's illegal and the CTIVD has said so many times before.

Instead of changing their act, in **November 2019** people from both AIVD and MIVD called the media in a joint effort, to complain about their supervisor TIB. They don't like to answer questions about their work to their supervisor, and although 98% to 99% of their tap requests are approved, sometimes involving eavesdropping on "millions of people", they complain to the media about the 1% in which their request is denied. [133] The spies don't mention anything about the other supervisor, CTIVD, that is accusing them every few months of illegal tapping. Apparently this is something they rather avoid publicity about.

December 2019: CTIVD says... Well, you can guess by yourselves by now [134].

June 2020: Something new happens! "AIVD and MIVD less often wanted to hack and eavesdrop wrongly." Secret Services that want to break the law *less often* are so special, that it's an actual headline in the news.[283] On the other hand: both AIVD[284] and MIVD[283] are also caught lying or withholding information to supervisor TIB, in order to get permission for "far-reaching actions" that would have been denied to them if all information was provided by them as they were obliged to do by law. But this doesn't seem to have consequence for anyone, besides the citizens that were spied on.

At last the government listens to me!

"Just because you're paranoid, doesn't mean that you're not being followed around by the police"...

I'm sure it's just coincidence. I was mailing a draft of this article to a dear friend, who was helping me correct my Dunglish. She had done quite a lot of work on it already, but as I kept discovering new dirt about Citybeacons (and writing new bits), it became a never-ending story. Then one day I did two things: I looked up some newspaper articles about predictive policing, without using a Tor browser. [135)] Then I wrote a paragraph about it, and malled it to her.

Within a few hours, I got a new follower on Twitter. Police chief and intelligence officer Frank Smilda is head of the Regional Information Organisation, specialisations: "Big data, predictive policing, social media".

I didn't post anything on twitter in the days before that could be interesting to him, one would say. Nothing about police, or the piece I was writing. Or maybe this police commissioner living in Groningen had a keen interest in my tweet about a school in Belgium, or the one about the Dutch media coverage of the situation in Catalonia, or my tweet about housing shortage in Berlin? (Rare coincidence, but I didn't tweet anything about the Netherlands that week)

I can't deny I felt a bit intimidated. Still, this is probably just a coincidence.

Commercial policing

What's more interesting: In many cases it's not the police nor the secret service that's monitoring you.

The line between commercial and state surveillance is blurring more and more.

Research by Buro Jansen en Janssen [136)] showed that the Dutch police are monitoring social media on a big scale. But the work is outsourced to commercial enterprises like Coosto, OBI4wan and HowAboutYou. These businesses scrape and mass-copy social media messages, so even messages that are deleted or set to private later, can still be analysed. With pseudo-scientific methods, messages are labelled positive, negative or otherwise. This "sentimental analysis" is then used to profile people, and further follow groups and individuals.

A new but big player in this market is Clearview AI. This startup scrapes social media profiles worldwide, and has already downloaded more than 3 billion portraits [137)] of people, mostly with their names attached, and extracted facial recognition data. Clearview

AI was hacked, and its client list is revealing. It sells biometric data to whomever is buying: shops, governments, banks, and other companies. This is all very likely to be very illegal. Despite this fact, by far the majority of the 2.200 customers are law enforcement agencies from around the world. Amongst them, according to leaked documents, a Dutch, unnamed governmental customer [138], which could be the police, although they deny that.

It's funny how Dutch media report on this, only now it's an international scandal, while most of the same media find commercial surveillance by Coosto, OBI4wan or HowAboutYou for the Dutch police not interesting at all.

7. Privacy breaches by others than the state

This lengthy article concentrates mainly on the Dutch government's role. I can't go very deep into other players. But as we all know, surveillance capitalism is much bigger than our governments alone. Google and Facebook have just one product, and it isn't a search engine or social media that they sell. The product is you. They harvest every move you make. They know more about what makes you tick than your mum does – they even know more about you than yourself. That knowledge, that data, is what they sell. Advertisers pay billions of dollars for it, and use it to make you do things you wouldn't have done if they hadn't.

We all think that we can resist those annoying ads. And we're all wrong. The 110.000 employees in the Dutch advertisement industry [139] don't get paid every day because their work is futile.

Also, big data is not just about manipulating you to buy stuff you don't need. In the hearings concerning Cambridge Analytica, we learned that Facebook data were used to help elect Trump and deliver Brexit. [140]

Still, many people feel brand loyalty, and think that the companies that build their apps are trustworthy. "They are too big to play around. And if they would make a mistake, our government will intervene!" Well, wouldn't that be great if it were true.

The little riot around Cambridge Analytica [140] showed what we can expect from both our politicians, and Zuckerberg et all. [141] In the hearings in US senate and European parliament we had politicians ask questions like: "Why am I suddenly seeing chocolate ads all over Facebook? Do I have as many friends as I think I do?" Zuckerberg barely answered them, and when the formal interrogation bores him, he decides it's enough. Mark tells the European Parliament "it's already 15 minutes past time" and just leaves. [142] Meanwhile our government's privacy watchdog, the one you hope that has sharper teeth and more knowledge, is so incredibly understaffed it's basically paralysed and cries for help in the media. Similar to 2018, the Autoriteit Persoonsgegevens received 27.800 complaints in 2019, investigated only 138, and imposed a fine or other sanction in just 25 cases. Less than one thousandth of the number of formal complaints. [143]

So, how about big corporations? Can we trust those? Can we assume that fear of reputational damage will keep them in check? Surely they have too much to lose, to share our data with unknown others?
This piece is long enough as it is. But just let me give one example: Grindr. This dating app, geared towards gay, bi and trans people, of course knows an enormous amount of very personal things about its users, not the least of which is their sexuality. The Norwegian Consumer Council found out Grindr shares your data with nineteen third party companies. Many of these nineteen companies share it again, one of them even with 170 more partners. One of these 170 companies shares it yet again-with 4259 others. Whether those 4259 companies also share your data is not known, but, logically, the likelihood is fairly high. [144].

Grindr transmitted personal data to
19 third party companies

MoPub - One of Grindr's partners, reserves the right to share your personal data with
170 partners

AppNexus - One of MoPub's partners, reserves the right to share your personal data with
4259 partners

(Image used with kind permission of researcher Øyvind Kaldestad and Forbrukerrådet Norway.)

Do I need to remind you that 73 countries persecute LGBTIQ? Countries you might be visiting on a holiday? Still, our government didn't stop Grindr from sharing data about your sexuality. Data that can easily lead anyone to your identity, according to the researchers. [145]

Grindr is no exception. The researchers consider this "representative of widespread practices in the ad tech industry."

Governmental protection of citizens against unlawful privacy breaches is nothing but a joke, a pipe dream.

Replacing originality with discipline

AI and deviant behaviour

ViNotion builds audience-tracking cameras for Citybeacons, Living Lab Stratumseind and others. They claim their cameras detect "deviant behaviour" (in a statement [146]) that must bring some envy to psychologists and developers of the Diagnostic and Statistical Manual of Mental Disorders, if you permit me some cynicism. Although the software is really incredible smart! The same statement continues with: "ViSense software [by ViNotion] is designed to detect only persons, and to not give false notifications about trees or animals"... I mean: wow! So sophisticated they can determine from a distance if I'm having a psychotic episode, *and even* if I'm a tree or not!)

Sorama also claims to be able to detect deviant behaviour with their microphones, and so do many more surveillance and smart city companies.

But what exactly is *deviant behaviour*?

In 1974 the former Stichting Pandora published this poster, containing only letters on a reflective, mirror like surface, that said: "Ever met a normal person? So... Did you like it?"

What is deviant behaviour?

Psychologists, pedagogues, anthropologists and sociologists around the globe have heated discussions about that question. [147] Most of course say that there are different types of deviant behaviour: not just unlawful behaviour, but also deviation of cultural norms. But when can you call behaviour normal, and when can you call it deviant? It's at least as difficult as defining the cul-

90

tural norms themselves. Cultural norms are subjective by nature, are changing all the time, and are by definition never shared by all. Also, dominant cultural norms exclude ideas in subcultures, and when enforced they exclude minorities. The political ideology that thinks enforcing all dominant cultural norms on everyone is a good idea, is called fascism.

Even if you would close your eyes for that, and would totally let go of the cultural aspect, deviant behaviour is almost impossible to define (let alone the causes). Psychiatrists try to agree on some common definitions in the DSM (Diagnostic and Statistical Manual of Mental Disorders), that's not meant to label everyone, but only meant to diagnose people that ask for help. Even so, many colleagues strongly oppose their proposals. [148]

It's funny how some software engineers apparently know much more about human behaviour than anthropologists and psychiatrists do. Their employers of course don't want long and deep discussions, they want a quick solution they can sell. Algorithms are written that label certain behaviour as "deviant" without much thought.
Like the aforementioned Sorama that defines running on the side walk as deviant behaviour, even "aggression". [28]

Decisive prejudices

Sometimes organisations say that they are aware of the fallibility of automated decisions, which is of course a good first step. For instance the police force claims [149] that smart solutions and algorithms just help them filter big data, but the decisions are never only made by machines. And indeed, Sorama is proud to show that when a person runs on the pavement, the neighbourhood watch is alerted with a text message saying; "*aggression in sector xxx, please respond*", while nobody is fined or arrested automatically. There's still a neighbourhood watch and even a police car needed to go and check if that should be done.
But of course this is fake-humanisation of machine decisions. If I'm the one happily jogging in Strijp S, it's still a machine that

91

decides if people must watch and check me for aggression. A machine that makes the first decision about what's deviant and what's not, if I'm to be harassed by police or neighbourhood watch or not. It's also a machine that decides when my behaviour is NOT dangerous. In an AI environment, there is far less chance that security or police will check a situation if the system didn't flag it.

The machine makes these important decisions, which are literally based on the prejudices of the person that wrote the algorithm. We are all at least a little bit trained to see through the prejudices of a person. But although some organisations claim to be aware of 'fallibility' of AI, in everyday reality most people (and most security, police etc.) think that computers "can't make human mistakes". Often the outcome of some algorithm is thus perceived almost like the voice of god.

Even worse is Artificial Intelligence, e.g. machine learning, which consists of algorithms that improve themselves, mostly without human control. A sharp example of what this can lead to is Tay Tweets. Tay was a chatbot built by Microsoft that was meant to have innocent conversations with people on Twitter, driven by AI. The bot was supposed to learn to engage with people through "casual and playful conversation." But within only one day of that machine learning, Tay turned into a deeply racist and sexist bot, tweeting racial slurs and telling people that dictators were great. [150)

Since the last breakthrough in Artificial Intelligence
the future was no longer what it had been

The problem is: Machines don't have a conscience. Also: they can't really think, they can only repeat what's fed to them. We are handing power from us, over to machines, while the algorithms that are fed to them, are almost always trade secrets that we can't check.

Another funny thing. While machines are programmed to flag everything they don't usually encounter as "deviant", something else that's not encountered very much, and which is deviant by nature, is *innovation*.

Another one: *Originality*. Are you sure it's a good idea to erase that from society?

Philosophical questions

As long as there are people who think they have the right to rule others, there has been violence. In the Middle Ages, this violence was sharp and displayed publicly. Convicts and especially rebels were tortured and beheaded on the main square, or even drawn and quartered.
But when kings fell and factories rose, capitalism demanded a very different form of control and power.

The panopticon was a nineteenth century form of prison architecture that was designed to discipline its inmates. There are still some in use. In a panopticon, inmates are separated from each other. More importantly: all prisoners can be observed at all times by a single, unseen security guard. There is no place for them to hide, not even in a cell or on the toilet. The isolated inmates know this, but they don't know *when* they are being watched and when not. The panopticon was invented by one of the founders of liberalism e.g. capitalism, the philosopher Jeremy Bentham. He meant to discipline prisoners. His reasoning was that because they don't know when they're being watched, they would start to behave as if they were all the time.

More than a century later, philosopher Michael Foucault used these prisons as a metaphor for the disciplinary "panopticism" that arose in all of society, (not accidentally) together with capitalism. [151] Although modern prisons, schools and work floors are very different from the brute violence that central powers used to discipline citizens in the Middle Ages, Foucault doesn't consider panopticism better or more humane. Like the panopticon, it hides power from view. It makes people malleable, and the violence that forces them to adapt to another's will is still there, but it's hidden behind schedules, 360-degree feedback, managers, CCTV, flexibilisation of employment and housing, and representativeness. As we never know when someone is watching us, we discipline ourselves. Losing a large part of our personality and interconnectedness in the process, to a life of servitude, permanent adaptation and alienation. A life that we can only maintain by seeking permanent distraction through entertainment, and energise with fear of the other; of the outcasts and the misfits: the scapegoats. Fear that leads to even more demand for discipline.

Clubbed into submission

Philosopher and sociologist Willem Schinkel gives a clear modern day example of this self-reinforcing mechanism in discipline, or "prepression", as he calls it, when he talks about integration. He says (in my words): Immigrants, unemployed, convicts, people who had cancer: they have something in common. The government wants them to integrate or even reintegrate, as 'they are outside society'. Schinkel asks rhetorically: "Where are those people then? In Belgium? At sea?" Of course that's nonsense. All those people are as much a part of society as heterosexual cis whites with a good education, health and a well-paid job are.
When you say someone needs to integrate to be part of society, you are in fact expelling that person from society. By saying 'minorities need to integrate' (meaning assimilate) 'so they can fully participate in society', we actually create a policy with which our society tries to purify itself.
The question of integration, is in reality rooted in dystopian thinking. It's rooted in looking upon our society as something finished and ideal, but threatened by elements from the outside: too many refugees, too many elderly, junkies, illiterates, anti-racists, rac-

ists, fraudsters, school dropouts, chronically ill, etcetera. [152] [153]
Asking people to integrate, is telling them they are not, and never will be, part of "us". No matter how much you try to integrate, you will always be an immigrant / ex-cancer patient / ex... You can never be disciplined enough. In this view, to discipline someone, whether by prisons, schools or cameras, is the actual declaration of *othering* of a body.

Enough of these complicated philosophies, and back to Foucault's notion of discipline by the guard that can see everything. It almost seems a cosmic joke that Foucault died in 1984, as this is also the title of the famous book by George Orwell about a dystopian future. Orwell fought as a volunteer during the Spanish Civil War, against Franco's fascism and Stalin's totalitarianism. But still, modern authorities seem to think his book is not a warning but a manual.

The main characters in the Dutch privacy drama

Who were the key figures in the Dutch camera-boom?

Cameras popping up like mushrooms

The Netherlands are in the middle of a quick transition from relatively few CCTV cameras towards an abundance of smart cameras and other sensors in the streets. In 2003, of the 489 Dutch municipalities [154] only 3% had more than 20 security cameras installed. Just two cities, Heerlen and The Hague, had more than 60. Half of the municipalities had no cameras at all, and of the cities with cameras, half of those weren't even digital. [155]
We don't know how many cameras are installed now; there is no national registration, not even of government owned cameras, let alone (semi) privately owned ones. Weblog Sargasso did extensive research in 2013, and estimated that there were 1 million in public places. [156] Research by DSP in 2014 estimated 1,5 million. [157]

A local example: In 2008 the total number of cameras on the streets of Eindhoven was twenty-one. [158] In 2013 the university campus of Eindhoven alone had eleven of them. In 2018, just this campus alone had two hundred forty-five cameras. [159]

The question arises: What is the motivation for this incredibly fast conversion towards a surveillance society?

Main Characters: Alexander Sakkers

Alexander Sakkers, now retired, was the mayor of Heerlen (2000-2003) and Eindhoven (2003-2007). Heerlen was the first Dutch town to have 100% camera surveillance coverage of the city centre. The motivation for this was Operation Heartbeat, an operation which mayor Sakkers was not only politically responsible for, but personally invested in.

Operation Heartbeat was the tough approach towards drug addicts that combined repression and care. "Healthcare was not operating in isolation any more, but involved in a repressive approach. (...) Splendid achievements. 'Sometimes we made 60 or 70 arrests in one day. We would push them towards the police trailers with violence. Shopkeepers were thankful and came to help us in person.' [160]"

In 2003 alone, one thousand eight hundred restraining orders were handed out to people, forbidding them to enter the city centre. But mayor Sakkers wanted more: he used cameras to record the license plates of slowly driving cars in the neighbourhood of alleged sex workers. He then wanted to send automated letters to their home addresses, warning them and maybe their families that next time they would be fined for solicitation—although this is not punishable by Dutch law. [161] His plan didn't work out though, as the RDW, the government service for license plate registration, refused to give out the names and addresses as it's illegal to do so. Sakkers tried to get the names and addresses anyway by asking the CPB (now: Autoriteit Persoonsgegevens) for approval, but they agreed with the RDW. [162] Then, despite the advice, Sakkers tried to force the RDW in court, but he lost the case. [163] An appeal was of no use either. [164]

Sakkers took every legal possibility to get rid of privacy boundaries that got in the way of his plan. But most privacy violations are not even done consciously. According to research in 2003, most municipalities that used surveillance cameras had barely any idea of the privacy laws they had to follow. [165] As you already saw, not much has changed since then. We will also find that not all 'lack of knowledge' is accidental: sometimes corruption is involved.

But first: back to Heerlen. So in the slipstream of Operation Heartbeat, Heerlen became the first Dutch city to have 100% camera coverage of the city centre. In 2003 Sakkers placed an order for smart cameras for the project with VCS International BV, worth 3 million euros. The deal should have been granted after a public tender, but the contract was directly awarded. Sakkers knew the company's executive director personally from a conference, but didn't mention that to the city council. There were a lot of questions about this deal, as wrong numbers seem to have been presented by Sakkers to the council, and the deal seemed to be violating European tendering rules. [166]

The turmoil increased when Sakkers was asked to enter the Board of Directors at VCS only two years later. By then he was already major of Eindhoven, and the city had also placed a huge order with VCS [167]. Sakkers accepted the position of director with VCS[168], but when the pressure from Eindhoven's city council and even national parliament grew, he rethought and refused[169]. Quite a lot of people were surprised when a formal investigation concluded that the Heerlen deal with VCS was indeed a violation of the law, but that it was the fault of unnamed lower officials, while their boss (and the political authority responsible) mayor Sakkers was 'not to blame'. [170]

VCS International BV didn't change its policies, although it changed its name to VCS Observation after the upheaval. In 2010 they hired police chief Hans Lesscher.

When Lesscher started to work as the police chief of Flevoland in 2006, as police commissioner of Almere, the province had just one working surveillance camera. [171] When he left four years later, the city centre of Almere had practically 100% camera coverage.

The camera system that was used is Coppweb [172] by VCS [173]. One could easily think Lesscher is rewarded for this, because he leaves Almere to become managing director of VCS. [174] But this time there is no turbulence in the media; maybe we consider it normal by now, or maybe most journalists are lazier than we would like.

Alexander Sakkers meanwhile, didn't fulfil his full time as mayor of Heerlen, neither did he as mayor of Eindhoven. There was another upheaval when a wethouder was accused of fraud and the sound recordings of an enquiry into his integrity went missing, under the responsibility of Sakkers. [175] When the Dutch parliament started to ask questions about Sakkers' camera deal in Heerlen, the mayor called the paper and publicly warned everyone that "the point on which I can't accept any more allegations, is coming closer fast." [176]

The next year, Sakkers left office prematurely for a job as chairman with Transport en Logistiek Nederland. This is where Sakkers starts to work with police chief **Peter van den Ende** and entrepreneur **Otto Vroegop**. Together they start **Secure Lane** [177], a project that installed smart cameras at truck stops. Its AI system warns the police when it thinks it spots "deviant behaviour".
Sakkers and Van den Ende present it as a huge success. [178] However, after installing the camera system on multiple routes, the cargo theft in the Netherlands actually increased: 600 cases in 2008, 1.141 in 2010. [179] Sakkers and Van den Ende are not impressed by those facts and use quite an original argument to cover their tracks. They admit that security cameras don't really end crime at all, but just relocate it: the so-called "waterbed effect." [180] But they don't present this as a reason to start doing something else and more efficient against crime. On the contrary, they both use the waterbed effect as an argument for 100% camera coverage of "the underlying network of roads", meaning: every road and parking place in the Netherlands [178] (to begin with) so the 'water' can't go anywhere without being noticed any more (and neither can you).

Research found no positive effect of camera surveillance

At the start of the camera boom, yearly nationwide research was done into the effectiveness of security cameras employed by local authorities. The fourth and final national report [181] in 2010 concluded that NO overall positive effects could be measured. Of the 489 Dutch municipalities at that time, only nine areas in eight cities had done scientifically valid evaluations. Three of those were inconclusive, three showed a *positive*, and three a *negative* effect for objective safety. For instance Utrecht found a rise of incidents in areas with cameras, while the number stayed the same in areas without cameras. Police in Utrecht and Goes concluded that cameras are no deterrent for perpetrators. Moreover, in Goes expected effects were small to begin with, and weren't measured quantitatively either. The city's goal was "to give a feeling of safety and well-being to visitors. To prevent people from ruining the atmosphere." The effectiveness of reaching this goal wasn't even measured by asking people about their feelings or the atmosphere, but by asking the police what they thought about it. Still, according to the researchers the evaluation in Goes was scientifically valid. One can only imagine what the many invalid evaluations must have been like.

Main Characters: minister Ivo Opstelten

So, there's no measurable positive effects of camera surveillance in the Netherlands. The end report [182] that came out the same month, wrote: "Effectiveness of camera surveillance is difficult to determine, and sometimes not measurable at all. (..) In 2005, 25% of municipalities were still convinced that camera surveillance is more effective than other means. In 2009 this is only 10%. It's good that municipalities realise camera surveillance is no panacea."
Another conclusion: quite a lot of municipalities have no idea about the laws around camera surveillance. Some commit crimes daily, for instance by not involving the police at all when looking at the recorded footage. [183]

Somehow Ivo Opstelten, minister of Safety and Justice, presented exactly this report to parliament with the words: "The large majority of municipalities indicates that camera surveillance is a good complement on other measures. The researchers state that after ten years of camera surveillance in the public space, the conclusion is that camera surveillance works." [184]

Of course this was an absolute lie. But apparently nobody took the effort of closely reading the reports themselves. Minister Opstelten was sent home five years later, for misinforming parliament in another case. In 2017 he was also discovered to have been manipulating several reports to parliament, adjusting unwelcome conclusions by the Scientific Research- and Documentation Centre (WODC). [219][220] During his career Opstelten was awarded the Big Brother Award by Bits of Freedom three times, for "doing most to threaten personal privacy." [221]

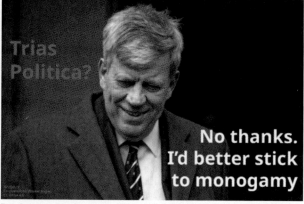

Text: Grutjes. Photo: Wouter Engler, [CC BY-SA 4.0] 222)

After presenting the conclusions of research to parliament as the opposite of what they were, no new research was done by the ministry. The number of cameras just kept on booming unhindered. In that, the rest of the world seems barely different from the Netherlands. Even though worldwide scientists have claimed for more than a decade that camera surveillance barely had any effect on nuisance or violent crimes, politicians decided to have them installed anyway. [185)

Main characters: minister Grapperhaus

Today, little has changed. Grapperhaus, current minister of Justice and Safety (yes, the ministry was renamed, cost: 32 million euros [186)]) tells us [187)] that no new limits to the use of AI in police work will be set by law, but that there will be "ethical reviews" in every development concerning AI. Of course you can't assess ethics if you don't decide first what your ethics are, but luckily Grapperhaus wrote to parliament: "research into ethical considerations for responsible use of AI within the law enforcement, was commissioned by the police." Although he does add a hyperlink to the research, apparently he doesn't really expect parliament to read the conclusions of the research itself, and indeed, the link does not work. If you search for it by name, you do find it though. There's a lot to be said about it, but let me just name the second requirement the research gives for any use of AI: "Transparency". [188)]

Grapperhaus names the research, giving the impression that everything the police and the ministry does is in accordance to it, but he refuses any transparency. The algorithms used are secret, he refuses to notify citizens, doesn't name commercial partners in AI, he doesn't even tell parliament exactly where AI is used. "Only a limited number of AI applications are used currently (..) For example, applications that facilitate the work of police officers but that do not have a significant impact on citizens. This *may* include searching through seized data carriers on images with image recognition to find a specific object." (Italics by me, not by Grapperhaus)

But what does Grapperhaus mean when he says "image recognition" on "seized data carriers" do "not have a significant impact on citizens"? He means facial recognition by AI, and not just on seized data carriers.

The database contains at least 2,2 million portraits of 1,3 million people, including many of innocent citizens. The database is not just used by Dutch police, as searches are done for foreign authorities as well. The AI software, named "CATCH", is not yet used in real-time "at the moment", according to Grapperhaus, but does use videos and images from security cameras, social media, anything any partner shares, any publicly available data, even police body cams. In 2019, about one thousand people were searched for using the system; only 98 led to a match. That's a success rate of only 10%, even if it would have led to 98 arrests – and it probably didn't, but we don't know, as no one is counting that number. [189] If you see that 1,3 million people are tracked a 1000 times a year to just (maybe) catch 98, the numbers become all the more absurd.

MPs asked Grapperhaus about the supervision of AI. The minister answered that theoretically the Inspection supervises the legitimate use of AI, including the prevention of discrimination by AI...however the Inspection has never done any research into this. When parliament asks the minister who then is responsible for monitoring ethical application of AI within the police, Grapperhaus answers: "The police."

In October 2019 the National Police organised Crxssing Bxrders: a big internal congress "in festival style" about innovation in police work. The official invitation flyer, asking police officers to come, said: "Crossing borders is what's needed to innovate. **Let's cross the borders of the conceivable, of ethics and of morality.**" [190]

Main Characters: Police chief Peter van den Ende

Police chief Peter van den Ende is seen as the most important driving force behind the transition of the Netherlands from a few old CCTV cameras to a country with a very high density of smart sensors. Van den Ende, commissioner of police in Eindhoven, was solely responsible for the procurement and use of cameras, sensors and microphones by the national police, [191] and advisor of the minister of Safety and Justice [192] But he was much more than that.

As we saw already when we talked about Stratumseind Living Lab, the supervisory board of umbrella-organisation DITSS is formed by important and trustworthy people: four majors, some-one working with the public prosecution and a police-chief. In the years 2009-2013 their project manager was police commissioner Peter van den Ende. [193] He is a busy man: he was also founder of RTR, an organisation that monitors police cameras. He was pro-ject leader of the public-private cooperation against criminality RPC Oost-Brabant [194], and together with former mayor Sakkers he was also the key figure in the start of Secure Lane. [195] And Van den Ende was not only working with the police, RTR, RPC and DITSS, but also had his own public/private triple helix enterprise, the non-profit foundation Criminee! (Translated: Crimeno!) Criminee!, with Van den Ende as CEO, was also one of the part-ners [196] that started **Living Lab Stratumseind**, his expertise being the implementation of smart cameras.

Another member of the supervisory board of DITSS was Otto Vroegop (2012-2015) [197]. He's managing director of iCOPP, a com-pany that builds software for smart cameras. iCOPP is again a triple helix organisation, consisting of The Hague Security Delta (yes, yet another triple helix organisation, how did you guess [198]), the national police, the police academy, and business. Van den Ende and Vroegop are actually friends and work together on many projects. Stratumseind was one of those, where DITSS, RTR, Criminee! and iCOPP joined forces [199].

In the summer of 2019 police chief Van den Ende was sen-tenced to a year imprisonment for fraud and accepting bribes. [200] Otto Vroegop was sentenced to eight months, for brib-ing him to use his software in smart cameras. [201]

Motivation for surveillance: corruption

The verdict makes one thing very clear: When Van den Ende was telling us that we need lots of cameras and sensors to be safe; his motive wasn't safety, but corruption.
Still, nobody has questioned any of the many decisions he took,

or the advice he has given. A multitude of cameras and sensors were installed because of him, but none of them were removed after his downfall.

Apparently our politicians and media don't really care why cameras and sensors are pointed at their citizens. If their chief advisor made up stories to sell them surveillance, if the main motivation for spying on citizens was corruption—well, whatever, that seems as good a reason for turning our society into a surveillance state as any other.

In the media we could read about the downfall of Van den Ende, but no criticism of surveillance was found anywhere. He was just named together with quite a lot of other policemen that were accused of corruption that year, without anyone asking questions about the substance of his work.

It's not customary in the Netherlands to fully name convicts. It may seem strange that we use Van den Ende's full name (in an article about privacy nonetheless!) instead of calling him "Peter van den E" as most media did. However, using shortened names is no absolute right. The media must thoughtfully balance the convict's rights to privacy–and rights to start a new life after having served his sentence–with the public interest.

As I said before, none of the decisions based on Van den Ende's crooked advice have been rescinded. Worse: there are still many videos[202] (with mayors, ministers and Chief Constable – soon to be chief of secret service AIVD – Akerboom as an enthusiastic public[203]) and websites[204] online in which Van den Ende is presented as a trustworthy name; the police chief that advices decision makers[205] to install as many sensors[206] and body cams[207] as they can. These videos and websites are still watched and taken seriously. Vroegop is even still in business, according to his LinkedIn page. It's important that decision makers come to realise that they've been had instead of just carrying on and basing their decisions on corruption.

Also, mindful of Karl Popper's "paradox of intolerance", we think that privacy is very important, but people who make it their core business to undermine the privacy of others, should not be able to hide behind the privacy they themselves chose to corrupt.

DITSS and RTR are still in business. RTR took over Criminee!, and Van den Ende's website[208] now points to RTR-NL. RTR has many activities, one of them[209] being the certification of public-private co-operations with a *quality mark for safety and trustworthiness...*[210]

Media seem as oblivious as politicians

The media, 'guard dogs of democracy', seem far from critical about smart cities.
The perception of Living Labs and on Citybeacons in Dutch media is mostly one of awe and cheering: "Hyper modern camera's will help police"[211] Eindhovens Dagblad headlines: "Citybeacons make Eindhoven smarter,"[212] and it writes: "a living lab, a place where new, sustainable and idealistic ideas can be put in practise"[213] And yes, there are some more critical articles too, but criticism of smart cities or Living Labs is nowhere near front-page news In the Netherlands, nor is investigative journalism it seems.

Overseas media see things differently. For instance the Guardian[214] has a completely different tone in its article on Stratumseind, Citybeacons, and sensors in Utrecht. It concentrates on the privacy aspect, noting that governmental control is lacking, and local authorities could not answer 17 out of 22 simple questions that the Guardian mailed them. It also concludes that smart cities lead to massive privatisation of public services. The headline: "'Living laboratories': the Dutch cities amassing data on oblivious residents."

It would be great if the article you are reading now could help local media take a more investigative and critical attitude towards this subject. But, although I would love to be proven wrong, my hopes are not too high.

Smart cities and the world

The development of smart cities is not happening in a void. In the world around us, the so-called smartness of our cities is not the only disruptive thing going on. In reality, the 'smartening' of cities is a relatively small change compared to the Big Two, although the three are interlinked.

Dear reader, a case for hopelessness.

1. Climate crisis

The first, biggest change going on around us is climate change. Although we hear about it in the daily news, most people still don't (want to) know how enormous and fast the change will be – and no one knows where it will end.

We all heard about the Paris agreement, which formalised a commitment to not let the temperature rise more than two degrees. And we all know that countries around the world are failing entirely to do what's needed to uphold that agreement: CO2 levels are rising instead of falling. They're rising fast.[215]

What most people also rather don't want to hear is that, according to the UN climate panel, even if we uphold the Paris agreement, **worldwide genocide** is to be expected.[216] To prevent this, temperatures can't rise more than 1.5 degrees. Should the temperature rise two or more degrees, hundreds of millions of people are predicted to die as a direct result, and not some 100 years from now but within the coming twenty years, according to the climate panel.

The UN panel is required to seek consensus for every report. Taking into account the not fully accounted for knock-on effects, climate scientists actually contend our reality will be far worse. Following the current, latest rise in CO2 levels, we will reach the two degrees threshold within the coming ten years[215], and we will be collectively slammed by the resulting, predicted genocide.

From an average temperature increase of two degrees (and well before that, on a smaller but increasing scale), the climate crisis will inexorably trigger mass animal extinction (which has already begun), with enormous droughts and desertification here, giant storms and flooding there, and failed harvests becoming routine. A spike of these types of climate extremes will lead to global food- and clean water shortages, which will in turn fuel massive numbers of environmental refugees. With literally hundreds of millions of people expected to die, resulting in the sudden, full halt of a highly interconnected global economy, the probability of *societal collapse* becomes disturbingly real.

2. Rise of fascism

The authoritarian right continues its muscular, global resurgence, even as I write. You might not agree with my heading, arguing that Trump, Johnson, Netanyahu, Erdogan, Kaczynski and Orbán are not true fascists, and indeed, they are not fascists in the classic sense. But bear with me, as with Bolsonaro or Salvini that point of view becomes far less easy to defend. We can agree at any rate on the reality of the rise of a new kind of dictatorship: "strongmen," who, while elected democratically, show nothing but contempt for everything that democracy was intended to be. This latest variant of the strongman shows particularly deep contempt for the rights of minorities, and little to no respect for facts, certainly not for that biggest, most inconvenient of facts, the climate crisis.

There is coherence to that logic. Strongmen thrive in crises. And they use that corresponding logic for their own profit, resulting in a race to hell. The more the climate changes, the more people feel uncertain. Insecure people will tend to vote more for strongmen with their empty claims of security. As more strongmen are elected, less is done to limit climate change, and the faster temperatures will continue to rise – which leads to more insecurity and an ever growing call for even more dictatorial rule. While climate change is not the only mechanism behind the rise of authoritarianism, it certainly contributes to it.

What do smart cities have to do with all of this?

To begin with, these fast global changes might say something about the futility of smartening up our cities. Indeed, some sensors in things like Citybeacons do measure air pollution, waste, temperature, and other climate variables that can help us understand climate change. So you could accordingly argue that at least this aspect of smart cities could help limit climate change. But then we forget how these sensors, and the data centres that store their data, need energy. At the moment, data centres in the Netherlands uses 3% of all available electricity; more than all wind energy in the country combined. When we add the energy needed for data traffic, we're already at 6%. The expectation is that this will rise to a staggering 50% of all available electricity by 2030 – which would mean that all "plans for energy transition are completely futile."[217]

Almost nobody thinks about this. There is no governmental policy. Some people hope we will miraculously find a way to bring energy levels down, although we use about twice as much energy for data every four years. But even if you forget about the enormous amounts of energy that smart cities eat, you can't claim that sensors will help solve the climate crisis. You would only say that if you believe that climate change and the accompanying environmental collapse could be prevented with technological means.

Well, I'm sorry, but tech won't cut it.

At the core of our capitalist system is growth. Capitalism simply can't exist without growth.
But our earth is not endless—far from it. It is very finite, with clearly confined limits. As long as we keep mining minerals and burning fuel to power up those high-tech sensors, even while entirely recycling everything and making an immediate and full transition to 100% green energy, we simply cannot grow infinitely within this, our only finite space.

The only possible answer to the climate crisis is to end capital-ism. This is not a socialist or some sort of lofty, lefty remark; it is cold, basic logic. We can't keep growing, and capitalism can't sur-vive without endless growth. We therefore need an alternative.

Instead of thinking (and acting very quickly) to develop other kinds of economies and social organisation, however, we put a lot of energy into smart cities, that are supposed to do...well, what exactly?

If you click around the internet a bit, this is what you'll find:

- "It is just so easy if you don't have to go and check if the waste container is full, but that instead your sensor sends you a message when the garbage truck needs to come."
  (And with that high tech "advance" we can fire most of our garbage collectors, a nice cost saving for the municipality that's not so nice for those people rendered redundant and jobless in the name of "convenience.")
- "Smart cities and the innovation that goes with it are good for economic growth!"
  (Oh. That's a pity. If we need anything, it is economic shrinkage, not growth. We shouldn't innovate within capitalism to make even more money out of the systematic killing of our environment, we should innovate, or rather rethink, our economic system from its root.)
- "Smart cities are good for safety!"
  (Well, actually, there's a lot of heated discussion[218] about whether that's true. But smart cities are unequivocally good for *control*.)
- "We respect your privacy!"
  (Well, of course you don't, otherwise you wouldn't be pointing sensors on me. What is meant is: "We will respect the privacy laws – which can't keep up with our develop-ments anyway– or we will find ways to circumvent them. At any rate we will continue the pretence that we respect and uphold the law!")

- Almost everywhere glossy videos and presentations claim
  that it's all "very good for citizens."
  (But if you ask how, you are met mostly with silence.
  Sometimes there is a small benefit, for instance free Wi-Fi,
  but then there's a catch in most cases, such as Wi-Fi
  sniffers that shred your privacy.)

In the end, smart cities are mostly good for two goals: making
money and controlling people. They are good for just two parties:
business and government, not for the people who populate them.

What we are essentially building with smart cities is the infrastruc-
ture for the easy management of our lives by (near) future authoritarian regimes. If Thierry Baudet or one of his mates comes to
power, there will be no possible escape, with that "smart" control
in place. If he's succeeded by someone worse, and the two thousand twenties turn out to be the new thirties, you can forget
about going into hiding, about avoiding the ovens. You can forget about your grandchildren visiting your generation's Anne Frank
house, as there won't be one to see. In the surveillance society,
even a temporary hiding place is pure fiction.

I strongly suspect it's not wise to trust any current government
blindly. But I am certain it's unwise to trust any and all future governments yet to come.

Autonomy

Many people don't like articles like this. The Dutch call this "doem-
denken", feeling that doomsday visions are better discarded, even
if they are true or will very probably come true. After all, they don't
make for very comfortable reading, do they?
OK, so let's forget about the macro level. Let's look at this at a
somewhat more personal scale.

Privacy isn't the only argument against a state of total con-
trol-by-sensors. Another one that is barely looked at is autonomy.

The smart city is not measuring your entire being just for the fun of it. It does so because it wants to influence you. Ending aggression with a perfectly timed waft of oranges and a happy colour of light, like in Living Lab Stratumseind. Or maybe you could be persuaded to buy more bullshit you don't need, by letting machines interpret your emotions and personality, and micro-adjust commercials accordingly.

'**Nudging**' has a friendly sound to it, but it's still about trying to manipulate[218] people to do something they didn't actually intend to do in the first place. And in some ways, that's actually worse[223] than a grim policeman, violently ordering you to do this or that, because with nudging you're made to do things *without even realising* that you're being nudged. That's how it works best.

You and I need autonomy as an individual. We need to be able to make mistakes without some authority seeing that and forever remembering every error we ever made. And you need privacy, too. Without it, your personality is simply not able to ever fully develop. There's more; you're unable to form meaningful personal relations with others, if everything you say and do and think is effectively public knowledge, and you feel watched all the time. You need space, space of your own, space with your friends and family, where no outsider or bot is lurking, where you won't be algorithmically registered, weighed, classified, or nudged. Automated surveillance and data mining are taking those necessities away from you at a very fast pace.

I'm not the only one saying this either. Maša Galič (PhD) concluded exactly this about Living Lab Stratumseind in her paper[224], and I dare say the same conclusion applies to Citybeacons, and to lots of other "smart" city projects.

Dalek vs Citybeacon

The similarity is uncanny. By the way, if they start a fight against each other, who do you think will win? Dalek 1.0 or Dalek 2.0?

Photo of Dalek by Tony Hisgett from Birmingham, UK [CC BY 2.0][225]
Photo of CityBeacon by Bas Grutjes

Progress

"It's just progress. You can't stop progress. What do you want, to go back to prehistoric times?" We hear that one a lot about our disappearing privacy and freedom.

It's important to note that this is a fallacy. It contains two parts.

The first one is that the direction our society takes, is inevitable, and that surveillance capitalism is our future if we want it or not. History is not a straight line, even although it might seem that way in hindsight.[92] When you know the outcome of any conflict of interests, it may seem that no other outcome could have been possible than the one we got, but of course that's not true. [104] History is going in all directions. It's all kinds of people, doing all kinds of stuff. Historians try to tell a story that explains why we are here now, without too much unnecessary detail. So they don't talk about your great-great-grandfather going to the toilet, but he did, and that had consequences too. Most historians tell the story of the victor, the dominant group, so you may think there was an incredible lack of women before the sixties, as you almost never hear about one of those creatures existing before that decade. You may think there were no black scientist or writers of any importance, not even in the past decades. [102] But you would be wrong.

Because we are used to thinking in straight cause-and-consequence lines, we tend to think our current system of values is something that has always been there, or that it has steadily grown on us in the past centuries. For instance the Dutch extreme right, seeing that women's rights are too enshrined in Dutch society to challenge them, call those rights typical for the "Western Jewish-Christian culture", in an attempt to weaponise this false claim into a stick to beat "invading" Muslims with. It is of course total nonsense: In France, up until 1970, you would get about 23 years less imprisonment if you would murder your wife in stead of a stranger. Up until 1991, raping your wife was no crime in the Netherlands. And did that cosy Jewish-Christian culture take a holiday in '40-'45?

"The line of progress is never straight", as Martin Luther King Jr. said. If you do imagine you see a line, there is no guarantee, nor law of nature, that this line will go on into the same direction in the future; you can make it change its course.

The second fallacy is that when someone doesn't like a particular development in society, he thus wants to go 'back to prehistoric ages'. Has our mindset really become so dystopian, that we can't imagine progress any more, towards a world that's friendly for people and planet? How is it that you think it's not possible for people to use technology to bloom, and enrich each other's human dignity? Are you sure technology must always be used like this: top down, used to accumulate power from the many to the few, used as weapons of distrust, used as weapons of manipulation and control?
Progress, you said?

113

Is resistance futile?

Well, yes, but no.

Many (if not most) people feel some resistance in their hearts against smart cities, online spying and other privacy breaches. But most are cynical about the option to stop "progress", as it is called. They feel overpowered. As a result, very few people organise themselves in a sustainable way, and street campaigns on this theme are rarely seen in the Netherlands.

Still, sometimes there are big outbursts of concern about privacy, like when a majority voted against the aforementioned "Sleepwet" in a referendum.

After the government lost that referendum, however, the state just said "well, whatever," made a few, minimal, cosmetic changes, and introduced the law anyway. And then nothing further happened, apart from some people tweeting angrily about it.

So resistance can *seem* futile. And that is exactly the reason why it can actually *become* futile.

People feel overwhelmed when they hear more about the seriousness of privacy concerns. The intrusions are so very massive in scale, the resistance against them so small, and the powers behind them so mighty, that it seems a waste of time to even think about it.

At the same time, many intrusions are packaged and sold very cleverly. While you won't notice many direct consequences in the short term, when you use Google, or Facebook, or your smartphone, you do immediately experience benefits: you find your way, new people, or info and diversion. What you don't actually experience is how your private movements, thoughts, and feelings–the intangibles that make up your very being–are being taken from you and sold to the highest bidder. It happens, but you don't get to see it directly, so why worry about something you can't see, something you can't even stop completely if you tried?

114

Well, there are many similarities between the fight for digital freedom and privacy, and the fight against climate change. Climate change is even more urgent, though most people don't perceive it that way, as you don't see sea levels rising before your eyes. There are many short-term benefits to ignoring climate change. If you want to put a stop to it, however, you will have to fight giant forces, including the government and crowds of people who prefer to put their heads in the sand after yelling abuse at you. And of course there are the multinationals, with more money for lawyers and lobbyists[226] than some countries have to feed their entire population.

There's no real surprise then to find hopelessness lurking, ever ready to ambush you, so you give up on everything.

TO PROVE YOU'RE A HUMAN, CLICK ON ALL THE PHOTOS THAT SHOW PLACES YOU WOULD RUN FOR SHELTER DURING A ROBOT UPRISING.

So is resistance futile?

Maybe not. There are successes in the fight against climate change as well as in the fight for privacy and digital freedom. And yes, sometimes it's one step forward and exactly that same step back, as with the Sleepwet referendum.

The Myth of Sisyphus by Albert Camus seems pretty apt:
Sisyphus is punished by the gods, by having to roll a big rock up a mountain for eternity. Every time when he's almost at the top, the boulder rolls down to the bottom again, and he has to start over. Albert Camus wrote a wonderful story about meaning and absurdity, as our lives have many similarities with the meaningless pushing of this heavy boulder by Sisyphus. Why not just give up?
Does the realisation of the absurd require suicide? Camus answers, "No. It requires revolt."
Sisyphus knows the futility of his effort and his existence, each and every time he walks down with heavy arms to collect the boulder. But he doesn't despair. "The struggle itself is enough to fill a man's heart. One must imagine Sisyphus happy".
The thing is, fighting is one of the most intense forms of feeling alive. It's not the goal that's the most compelling. If you would ever reach your goal you'd likely soon forget it. But the fight? That *is* life itself. (And besides, the constantly changing views on the way are magnificent.)

OK, I have to admit, the story of Sisyphus used to be my life's motto, and it's still important to me. But with the climate crisis it's no longer completely sufficient. Basically, what scientists predict is that we won't be rolling rocks up mountains for eternity. Soon, there may not be a mountainous society any more, but giant floods or maybe droughts that erode the top. What if 'the mountain', meaning society and our ordered lives, totally collapses? What do we do then, if we survive? As we sit beside that boulder, no mountain in sight, relieved from the punishment by the gods, our self-punishment is even greater: not rolling for eternity, but eternal boredom and uselessness will be our share. Not looking forward to goals that can *almost* be reached, not enjoying the

116

ride, but looking back on everything and everyone that was lost in the never-ending wastelands that we created. That we inflicted upon ourselves.

Maybe it will be hard to keep laughing about absurdity then.
But we're not there yet. Also, it's very important to realise that the climate crisis is **not a zero sum game**. (Well, that is not exactly true. It is a zero sum for every life form that goes extinct. But for the planet it isn't.) We don't have the choice between everything or nothing, we have the choice between few disasters, many disasters or a ton of disasters.
Every step you take, every piece of coal that stays in the ground, has effect, and leads to slightly less warming, less famine, less extinction. (Just remember your priorities. It's far more effective to eat a millionaire than to go vegan. This is not a joke[229].)

The same with smart cities; it's not a zero sum game. But it's certainly not going the right way, and the worst-case scenario is absolutely unbearable. **We must resist.**

A few years back protest against climate change seemed so small it could never have real impact. But last month more than 6 million people[230] took to the streets, everywhere in the world.
There aren't many protesters that defend privacy and digital freedom. But that might also change.

There is resistance against the smart city

Some resistance is technological. For instance, there are patterns that you can download and print on T-shirts[231] that will confuse facial recognition software, and many other methods.[232] The problem is that any technological 'solutions' are short lived: the software continues to improve and gets steadily harder to disrupt. In fact, your actions could help to train the software. Beyond its limited effectiveness, wearing special patterns or goggles does nothing towards outlawing surveillance technologies.
On the other hand, it does make people more aware, which remains very important.

There are some groups fighting for privacy and digital freedom. In the Netherlands, the most important ones are Bits of Freedom (who you'll read more about in this book) and Vrijbit. Apart from these quite professional organisations (some run by volunteers), there are also spontaneous initiatives, such as the three students who launched the referendum against the Sleepwet, and were soon supported by Amnesty International, thousands of volunteers, and eventually millions of voters.

Some protests are small but very cheerfully quirky. There are people who celebrate George Orwell's birthday (25th of June) every year, by putting paper party hats on surveillance cameras.[233]

Meanwhile, security remains very important, especially to journalists and activists. One of the open source tools developed to offer some shielding from the smart city is the Umbrella app.[6]

In the US, the protest against facial recognition is becoming so vocal and large-scale, that San Francisco introduced a law making facial recognition illegal[234]. As a result, other cities, states, and the federal government are thinking about following their example. This is no small step, knowing that half of all US adults were already in a facial recognition database by 2016.[235] It shows that sometimes, enormous changes that can seem like some kind of inevitable 'progress', can be revoked.

Critics of facial recognition lead astray by EU

Even the European Commission was thinking about a five-year moratorium, which was breaking news in the media. But after some pressure by security industry[236] the Commission totally dropped the plan two weeks later[237], without many media picking up that last story.

Shortly after that, The Intercept[238] published leaked reports that show that national police forces of ten EU countries are working together to push a plan for a network of facial recognition databases, so EU police officers can check databases of every EU country and even USA. The European Commission has already spent more than a million euros to "map the current situation of facial recognition in all EU Member States," with the aim of moving "towards the possible exchange of facial data." Privacy organisations are shocked. "Especially as some EU countries veer towards more authoritarian governments," says Edin Omanovic, advocacy director for Privacy International. Omanovic worries about a pan-European face database being used for "politically motivated surveillance" and not just standard police work.

Since April 2019, there's already an EU database containing fingerprints and facials of up to 300 million non-EU nationals, mostly migrants.[238] It's becoming a trend it seems, to erode peoples' rights by first attacking the civil rights of powerless minorities, before the erosion is normalised and applied to the general public.[239]

It's also tragic that a lot of Dutch media seem so oblivious about technology, and so biased towards the status quo. Mainstream media gave a lot of attention to a short-lived plan to forbid facial recognition, but none to the abandonment of that plan; citizens are appeased with a false confidence about their privacy, while their resistance is needed instead.

It doesn't have to be that way. German minister Seehofer plans to use automatic facial recognition at approximately 150 railways and airports, but awareness of privacy is much higher in Germany as it is in the Netherlands, and the plan is meeting so much resistance that it may result in the opposite. A large coalition of activists, media and politicians now demands a total ban on this surveillance technology.[240]

Hong Kong

Currently, the most notable and outspoken resistance is happening in Hong Kong. As you might know, Hong Kong is a semi-independent administrative region of China. Officially, only in 2047, will Hong Kong be fully integrated with China. But as Chinese interference with the region is already growing rapidly, 2014 saw a first, massive uprising, called the Umbrella Revolution. In 2019 we are witnessing a new surge of resistance.

Much of the protest is aimed at surveillance technology and general structure of the smart city. Protesters perceive the Hong Kong government as a puppet of China, and thus have no trust in any sensor aimed at them by that puppet. The protesters' tactics[241] are very advanced, and very coordinated. It seems some of them even carry liquid nitrogen[242] with them, ready at any moment to freeze canisters of tear gas thrown by the police. Their internal slogan is to "be like water". The protesters pop up in an area, block roads and buildings, and suddenly disperse by public transportation again when the police pressure gets too high. Then they pop up somewhere else.

There is extensive use of masks, helmets, shields, goggles, gas masks and umbrellas, and not just for protection against police violence, pepper spray and tear gas. These tools also help prevent identification by the omnipresent facial recognition cameras. People also make a point of wearing black at the protests, making it difficult to identify people from their clothes. Mobile supply stations distribute gear, train tickets, and non-black clothes so protesters can safely reach home without being recognised as a protester. Interestingly for this essay about the smart city of Eindhoven is what's happening to Hong Kong's lampposts: smart lights, installed by the city, were demolished by protesters as they were suspected to have facial recognition cameras attached. The Hong Kong government has acknowledged[243] that the lampposts have hardware to spy on citizens, but say the protesters' fears are unfounded, as some surveillance features, including license-plate recognition and audio visual surveillance, were 'disabled'. (Well, doesn't that make you think of home?)

In some ways, the surveillance state of Hong Kong is less totalitarian than Dutch society. People in Hong Kong can still legally buy anonymous burner phones, while we have to identify ourselves when buying a disposable SIM card. It was only last week that Hong Kong outlawed people who hid their identity with masks: something that is already forbidden in Dutch public transportation. Also, they can buy high-power laser pointers, which are forbidden here.

Hong Kong protesters use those pointers to damage surveillance equipment and make facial recognition difficult. The Western press doesn't really seem to consider why the protesters use lasers and umbrellas so much. But when you recognise that China will likely end the special status of Hong Kong well before 2047, you understand that when that happens, identified protesters will probably disappear en masse in concentration camps, or even face execution. Hiding your identity is already a matter of life and death.

The state reacts

Hong Kong police now uses water cannons that fire blue-dye water at protesters, so they can be tracked afterwards. In reaction to this the protesters now bring extra clothes, and solvents to clean their skin. The war-like situation is not just in the streets, but also online, where protesters use encrypted messengers to communicate, and apps that will lock their phones in case of arrest. Meanwhile someone, probably China, developed malware[244] to infect phones and spy on protesters, as was already discovered in 2014.

Although the degree of organisation is high, there is no leadership, similar to the now historic alter-globalisation movement and the Dutch squatters movement. The Hong Kong movement also shares tactics with Occupy, using hand gestures which are systematically repeated to send calls for equipment from the front line to the back. This tactic is essential given the scale; the biggest single protest up until now involved nearly 2 million citizens.[245]

Hong Kong protesters' tactics are spreading. While I'm writing this, massive protests erupt in Chile, against neo-liberal austerity, unchallenged climate change, and authoritarianism. While the state declared martial law, and patrols the streets with tanks, demonstrators use hundreds of laser pointers[246] to hinder facial recognition cameras on helicopters to prevent their identification.

There are people everywhere in the world actively resisting attacks on liberty and privacy; trying to build a peer to peer internet that doesn't need centralised servers which can be controlled; trying to build digital and physical spaces where they can be and communicate, without others trying to eavesdrop or control them.

But really, what can be dangerous about smart cities?

Aren't those protesters more dangerous?

As Ruben Terlou showed in his TV series[247], China is building a social credit system[248] driven by surveillance technology, AI, and facial recognition. With this system, if you walk through a red traffic light five times, you will be unable to get loans or insurance or train tickets[249], or rent a room, which basically bans you from the city.

This is entirely decided by an algorithm, without human interference, as a model who was featured on an advert on the city's buses recently discovered. The smart cameras weren't quite smart enough to see that her face was just ink printed on paper, on a passing bus, and not actually a real person. The system repeatedly put her on a blacklist for crossing red lights, even though the perceived infractions sometimes occurred at the same time in different parts of the city. Her fame will probably save her, but that can't happen for most people.

It's not just AI and facial recognition cameras that pry on every move, and classify every citizen. Even tourists are now obliged to install spyware on their phones in Xinjiang. It sends alerts to the police for using banned apps like WhatsApp, it shares the content of every text on your phone, and it searches your device for files against a target list, that are as diverse as music from a Japanese metal band, and copies of the Quran. Locals are made to install even more extreme spyware that label "many forms of lawful, every day, non-violent behaviour—such as 'not socializing with neighbours, often avoiding using the front door'—as suspicious."[250]

According to Chinese officials, the social credit system, operational in just a few cities so far had already barred **11,1 million people** from taking a plane by May 2018. Human Rights Watch[251] noted that same year that the first "preventive" arrests were made of people blacklisted by the social credit system, people who had not actually broken any law. People can actually be flagged for "owning a lot of books without being a teacher". The state plans for the social credit system to cover all of China by 2020, although that target will probably not be achieved in time.

Russia is following China's example. Moscow already has 160.000 CCTV cameras, of which 3.000 have facial recognition. The mayor of Moscow wants to install many more: the goal is 200.000 cameras with facial recognition. The first peaceful demonstrators (Mihail Aksel, and later Alena Popova) have been *automatically arrested* already.[252]

Moscow Is not alone. More democratic states are following. Belgrade[253] (Serbia, candidate EU member, where Chinese police[254] are now literally patrolling the streets) is already installing Chinese cameras with facial recognition, and even Germany[255] is experimenting with it.

Racism by machine

In China itself the smart city is used for systematic racism by the state.[256] Every movement of millions of people from the ethnic minority of Uyghur Muslims is tracked by smart cameras with facial recognition that lock onto their ethnic, 'racial' facial characteristics. According to The New York Times[257], Chinese start-ups like CloudWalk openly advertise this capacity: "If originally one Uyghur lives in a neighbourhood, and within 20 days six Uyghur appear," it said on its website, "it immediately sends alarms" to law enforcement. In February 2019, the database proved to be unsecured: everyone could find the names, IDs, addresses and current location of the 2,5 million people tracked[258].

Hikvision, not a start-up but a big company that also sells many cameras in the Netherlands[259], has proudly advertised their cameras to be able to automatically discriminate[260] Uyghur from

Han-Chinese. Hikvision installs facial recognition cameras in Dutch soccer stadiums at this moment. The Chinese multinational is a partner of TV magnate Talpa and Dutch soccer organisation KNVB[261], and a big sponsor of football club Ajax[262]. Ajax knows about Hikvision and their gross breaches of human rights, but they just don't care.[261]

New York Times[263] about Hikvision: "Automated racism".
Washington Post[264]: "In China, every day is Kristallnacht."
IPVM[265]: "AI-enabled ethno-religious persecution is the CCP's catastrophic invention of the 21st Century."

...KNVB[266]: "Smart cameras will help us to combat racism." Minister Bruins: "With microphones and facial recognition!"[267]
(I'm getting a headache)

Still we hear politicians, and even friends and neighbours, play down privacy concerns. Although all of them use curtains at home, they still say: "Whatever, I don't have anything to hide."
Is that so?

Concentration camps and harvesting people

Tracking Uyghur by AI and facial recognition cameras is not something that happens in a void of innocence. It has consequences. Researcher Adrian Zenz estimates that one million Uyghur are now detained[268] in Chinese concentration camps. The USA government claims the figure is even higher.

Eindhoven has a role in this, too. It is the leading force of the governance pillar[269] in LUCI, the international network of cities on (smart) urban lighting, including lampposts that contain cameras and other sensors like the ones in Living Lab or in Hong Kong. Like the ones used to follow all Uyghur...
Another member of LUCI profiting of the information Eindhoven and others, is the city of Guangzhou, China[270]. The city in which the Chinese government claims terrorist attacks by Uyghur took

place, which they use as an excuse to track the entire minority and lock-up at least a million of innocent citizens.

As I'm writing this, the independent China Tribunal[271] has reported to the United Nations about crimes against humanity against the Uyghur. The China Tribunal is a serious matter, chaired by Sir Geoffrey Nice QC, who was the prosecutor at the international criminal tribunal for former Yugoslavia, and who opened the case against Slobodan Milošević.
The message of the Tribunal[272] to the UN today was this:

> **The Chinese government is harvesting and selling organs from persecuted religious and ethnic minorities on an industrial scale.** Falung Gong members and Uyghur are "killed to order... cut open while still alive for their kidneys, livers, hearts, lungs, cornea and skin to be removed and turned into commodities for sale", the tribunal's final judgment said.

I don't even know what to say about this.
(Rutte and the city of Eindhoven did know what to say though:... nothing[273].)

The latest news from China is that the state started a governmental rape programme.[274] China appoints men from the majority of Han-Chinese, to young single Uyghur women, and to Uyghur women whose partner is taken and locked into concentration camps by the police. The Han-men get paid by government, and are forced upon the women as living partners, and even sleep in their beds. Uyghur women have no choice but to accept the situation, as they are declared to be Islamic extremists by the authorities if they refuse the men. According to human rights activists, mass rape is thus weaponised by the state for ethnic cleansing. The Chinese government does acknowledge the "pair-up programme", but claims it has nothing to do with rape. The Han-men are obliged to sleep in the beds with the Uyghur women, to "promote ethnic unity".

There is no escape for the women, or their real men. Not in the camps, not in their own beds at home, not in the streets where cameras and AI follow every move. One can only shudder to think about the next step.

Please end smart cities. Although the unbearable things happening in China are of course not to be entirely blamed on smart cities, smart cities ARE a totalitarian tool that no democrat should touch.

With love,
Bas Grutjes, anarchist rather than democrat, (because if electing your next oppressor could change anything it would already be illegal.)
www.grutjes.nl

PS: Cock-and-bull story

Every morning, the cock cheered for the rising sun.
"Just look at that!" it said: "The black of night, the red of dawn. Symbolic colours! Even nature is telling us our future is anarcho-syndicalism!"

But the young bulls didn't like complicated words, words that make your teeth feel like they're in the wrong order. A-n-archro-Cindy-kalism? Ha! They didn't want to have anything to do with extremism like that!
They liked to chew the cud, moo & boo about the elections, ruminate on the sexy movements of that heifer in the distance last week, and if they wanted to enjoy the exciting slight shudder that horror brings, they'd rather debate the chances of ever having to step outside the safety of their crates, instead the odds of revolution.

"There's a new butcher in town", one said to the other. "He says it's all over for the elite. I agree, we need some change around here!"
"Oh for crying out loud," said the other, "don't you see how populist that is? Don't vote for the guy, he doesn't offer any solutions,

and he's got no experience either. We'd better stick with the old geezer, who knows his trade."

"You guys are nothing but calves. Grow up!" said the third one. "We don't need ideologues with their political games! We need experts to lead us, or even better, a government that is rid of human mistakes!"

He went on, with a dreamy moo: "Haven't you heard about Artificial Intelligence? Full rationalization... How wonderful that would be: Deep Machine Learning sharpening the knives, and AI managing the abattoir! I would certainly die for it."

Sources

1) https://www.ed.nl/eindhoven/vijf-miljoen-voor-gezonde-levensstijl-in-regio-eindhoven~a94c801b/
2) https://www.ed.nl/eindhoven/victoria-park-in-eindhoven-wordt-living-lab~a0ab585e/
3) https://hub.beesmart.city/city-portraits/smart-city-portrait-eindhoven
4) https://www.tue.nl/universiteit/faculteiten/bouwkunde/onderzoek/smart-cities-program/collaboration/living-labs/
5) https://www.heijmans.nl/en/news/heijmans-and-philips-start-work-smart-lighting-eindhoven/
6) https://secfirst.org
7) https://vng.nl/files/vng/nieuws_attachments/2018/principles-for-the-digital-city_20181025.pdf
8) http://www.citybeacon.info
9) https://data.eindhoven.nl/explore/dataset/citybeacons0/information/
10) https://www.slideshare.net/webwinkelvakdag/big-data-in-eindhoven-realiteit-en-ambitie
11) https://www.ed.nl/eindhoven/makers-city-beacons-in-eindhoven-dit-is-nog-maar-het-begin~a256f974/
12) https://nl.wikipedia.org/wiki/Algemene_verordening_gegevensbescherming
13) https://www.eindhoven247.nl/nl/nieuws/jaaroverzicht-2017/out-of-home-media-krijgt-zicht-op-data
14) https://www.ndr.de/nachrichten/netzwelt/Nackt-im-Netz-Millionen-Nutzer-ausgespaeht,nacktimnetz100.html
15) https://fd.nl/economie-politiek/1207927/een-sensor-op-elke-straathoek

16) http://www.eindhoven247.nl/nl/nieuws/archief/smart-city-eindhoven-lanceert-city-beacons
17) https://www.security.nl/posting/580545/Camera's+in+reclameborden+voorlopig+uitgeschakeld
18) https://www.trouw.nl/opinie/die-camera-s-mogen-gewoon-nlet~b7a0d982/
19) https://autoriteitpersoonsgegevens.nl/nl/nieuws/ap-informeert-branche-over-norm-camera%E2%80%99s-reclamezuilen
20) https://innovationorigins.com/nl/smart-society-eindhoven-de-mogelijkheden-van-citybeacons/
21) https://www.eindhoven247.nl/nl/nieuws/nieuws-archief/smart-city-eindhoven-lanceert-city-beacons
22) https://pogue.blogs.nytimes.com/2007/01/04/04pogue-email/
23) https://podcastluisteren.nl/ep/Rush-Talk-Impact-van-innovatie-Rush-Talk-98-Eindhoven-een-stad-vol-sensoren
24) https://www.ed.nl/eindhoven/citybeacons-eindhoven-op-zwart-door-failliet-bedrijf~a1d5637d/
25) https://www.intel.com/content/dam/www/public/us/en/documents/events/iotswc/iotswc-demo-abstracts.pdf
26) https://www.intelrealsense.com/
27) https://www.intelrealsense.com/coded-light/
28) https://youtu.be/xXbCloUUNTY
29) https://www.intel.sg/content/www/xa/en/internet-of-things/videos/city-beacon-master-video.html
30) https://customers.microsoft.com/en-IN/story/749839-citybeacon

31) https://www.kvk.nl/zoeken/?-source=all&q=Hendrik%20Andriessenlaan%203%203055WX%20Rotterdam&start=0&site=kvk2014

32) https://www.eindhoven247.nl/nl/nieuws/jaaroverzicht-2018/digitalisering-van-buitenreclame-zet-door

33) https://sensorpilot.nl/

34) https://www.facebook.com/LivingLabStratumseind/posts/2079771915434582

35) https://www.brainport.nl/ditss/mensen

36) https://www.brainport.nl/ditss/wat-is-ditss

37) http://raadsinformatie.eindhoven.nl/user/bdocument/env=help/action=showannex/gdb=687/Bijlage_1_-_Nota_Digitalisering_van_de_stad.pdf

38) https://pure.tue.nl/ws/portalfiles/portal/113636903/Master_Thesis_Edoardo_Gualandi.pdf

39) https://www.securitymanagement.nl/ditss-de-successen-en-uitdagingen/

40) http://www.vcsobservation.com/actueel/nieuws/veiligheid-waarborgen-met-gezichtsherkenning-test-bij-grote-gemeenten/

41) https://sivv.nl/ditss-partner/

42) https://sivv.nl/deelnemer/

43) http://www.stopwapenhandel.org/node/1880

44) http://www.stopwapenhandel.org/sites/stopwapenhandel.org/files/Border-Wars-Report-web1207.pdf

45) https://www.passant.info/partners/

46) https://www.passant.info/smokkelaars-en-vluchtelingen-opsporen-met-slimme-cameras/

47) https://www.cursor.tue.nl/achtergrond/2018/oktober/week-4/smokkelaars-en-vluchtelingen-opsporen-met-slimme-cameras/

48) https://www.iottechexpo.com/europe/wp-content/uploads/2018/06/13.45-Tinus-Kanters.pdf

49) https://hetccv.nl/fileadmin/Bestanden/Onderwerpen/Grote_steden/netwerkdagen_eindhoven_living_lab.pdf

50) https://www.bigdata-expo.nl/programma/big-data-eindhoven-realiteit-en-ambitie

51) https://metropoolregioeindhoven.nl/actueel/ons-nieuws/nieuwsarchief/wat-kan-big-data-betekenen-voor-gemeenten/ll-trillion-2015

52) https://www.bnsp.nl/wp-content/uploads/2017/10/Presentation-LL-sept..pdf

53) https://docplayer.nl/54064666-Werk-en-met-sensoren-gewoon-doen-tinus-kanters-projectmanager-living-lab-stratumseind-eindhoven-gemeente-eindhoven-ditss-juni-2017.html

54) https://www.verkeerskunde.nl/Uploads/2017/8/ViNotion-Uitnodiging-Seminar-2017.pdf

55) https://rockproject.eu/uploads/news/documents/y0dLxcKYSLkQLBe5cwM6KxdVglVP-tUNtjCZQ9swo.pdf

56) Aardobservatie Op De Kaart, The Hague Centre for Strategic Studies 2016

57) https://ziladoc.com/download/report-as-pdf-11_pdf

58) https://www.bigdata-expo.nl/nl/sprekers/tinus-kanters

59) https://www.smartdatacity.org/stratumseind-living-lab/

60) https://innovationorigins.com/nl/stratumseind-de-datastraat-van-eindhoven/

61) https://decorrespondent.nl/5585/zo-simpel-is-het-voor-een-journalist-om-de-persoonlijke-data-van-miljoenen-te-bemachtigen/171772260-d650a506

62) https://research.tilburguniversity.edu/en/publications/surveillance-privacy-and-public-space-in-the-stratumseind-living-

63) https://nl.wikipedia.org/wiki/Holocaust_in_Nederland#Aantal_en_percentage_slachtoffers

64) https://www.verzetsmuseum.nl/museum/nl/tweede-wereldoorlog/begrippenlijst/achtergrond,aanslag/amsterdamse_bevolkingsregister

65) https://jck.nl/nl/longread/geschiedenis-van-de-joden-amsterdam

66) https://www.bright.nl/nieuws/artikel/4822091/gezichtsherkenning-europese-unie-commissie-regelgeving-gezicht-herkenning

67) https://autoriteitpersoonsgegevens.nl/nl/onderwerpen/cameratoezicht/cameratoezicht-op-openbare-plaatsen

68) https://www.bitsoffreedom.nl/2019/11/29/amazons-rekognition-toont-zijn-ware-gezicht/

69) https://creativecommons.org/licenses/by-nc-sa/4.0/deed.nl

70) https://www.theguardian.com/technology/2017/sep/07/new-artificial-intelligence-can-tell-whether-youre-gay-or-straight-from-a-photograph

71) https://www.amnesty.nl/encyclopedie/homoseksuelen-homofobie-homohaat

72) https://www.nrc.nl/nieuws/2018/06/18/de-burger-moet-kunnen-weten-hoe-de-misdaadvoorspeller-werkt-a1606978

73) https://www.rijksoverheid.nl/regering/bewindspersonen/ferdinand-grapperhaus/documenten/kamerstukken/2020/02/18/tk-beantwoording-schriftelijke-vragen-ai-bij-de-politie

74) https://www.nrc.nl/nieuws/2015/08/22/het-misdrijf-is-al-ontdekt-voor-het-gepleegd-is-1525496-a270899

75) https://www.chicagomag.com/city-life/August-2017/Chicago-Police-Strategic-Subject-List/

76) https://time.com/4966125/police-departments-algorithms-chicago/

77) https://web.archive.org/web/20190608190638/https://www1.nyc.gov/assets/adstaskforce/downloads/pdf/ADS-Public-Forum-Comments-NAACP-LDF.pdf

78) https://www.aclu.org/blog/criminal-law-re-form/reforming-police-practices/predictive-polic-ing-software-more-accurate?redirect=blog/speak-freely/predictive-policing-soft-ware-more-accurate-predicting-policing-predict-ing-crime
79) https://www.amnesty.org/en/latest/news/2016/12/salil-shetty-speech-techfest/
80) https://www.aclu.org/other/statement-con-cern-about-predictive-policing-aclu-and-16-civil-rights-privacy-racial-justice
81) https://www.nrc.nl/nieuws/2018/06/18/de-burger-moet-kunnen-weten-hoe-de-misdaad-voorspeller-werkt-a1606978
82) https://wetten.overheid.nl/BWBR0022463/2019-07-01#Paragraaf2_Artikel11
83) https://marcschuilenburg.nl/wp-content/uploads/2018/10/PredictivePolicingStrafblad.pdf
84) https://www.rijksoverheid.nl/regering/bewindspersonen/ferdinand-grapperhaus/documenten/kamerstukken/2020/02/18/tk-beantwoording-schriftelijke-vra-gen-ai-bij-de-politie
85) https://nlaic.com/coalitiepartners/
86) https://www.hrw.org/asia/singapore
87) https://www.straitstimes.com/singapore/using-artificial-intelligence-to-fight-crime-and-ter-ror
88) https://ditss.nl/bezoek-singapore-po-lice-force/
89) https://www.theguardian.com/uk-news/2018/may/05/welsh-police-wrongly-identify-thou-sands-as-potential-criminals
90) https://www.bbc.com/news/uk-51237665
91) https://gdpr-info.eu/art-9-gdpr/
92) https://chomsky.info/20150922/
93) https://fd.nl/economie-politiek/1207927/een-sensor-op-elke-straathoek
94) https://creativecommons.org/licenses/by-sa/2.0/
95) https://www.eindhoven365.nl/_asset/_pub-lic/Documenten/Jaaroverzicht-2016-Eind-hoven365_247.pdf
96) https://www.eindhoven247.nl/nl/wat-we-doen/evenementen
97) https://www.facebook.com/pg/Eindhovenisking/photos/?tab=albums
98) https://www.facebook.com/Eindhovenisking/posts/2030219923772310
99) https://dataschool.nl/deda/
100) https://eindhoven.raadsinformatie.nl/document/6599465/4#search=
101) https://www.eindhoven247.nl/nl/nieuws/jaaroverzicht-2017
102) http://www.theblackarchives.nl/over-ons.html
103) https://vinotion.nl/nl/producten/visense-crowddynamics/
104) https://lauraleeauthor.wordpress.com/2015/07/30/history-as-a-straight-line/
105) https://eindhoven.raadsinformatie.nl/document/2666183/1
106) https://data.eindhoven.nl/explore/dataset/citybeacons0/information/
107) https://innovationorigins.com/nl/smart-society-eindhoven-de-mogelijk-heden-van-citybeacons/
108) https://www.nu.nl/tech/5967571/gezichtendatabase-van-politie-bevat-fo-tos-van-13-miljoen-mensen.html
109) https://tweakers.net/nieuws/153122/autoriteit-persoonsgegevens-ontving-20000-pri-vacyklachten-sinds-avg.html
110) https://www.computeridee.nl/nieuws/helft-nederlanders-wil-cameras-met-gezichtsherk-enning-in-openbare-ruimtes/
111) https://tweakers.net/nieuws/158640/politie-kreeg-onterecht-toegang-tot-beelden-mi-lieucameras-gemeente-amsterdam.html
112) https://nos.nl/artikel/2250767-politie-wil-zakkenrollers-en-plofkrakers-vangen-met-data.html
113) https://www.rtlnieuws.nl/columns/column/4773721/menno-snel-belastingdienst-toe-slagenaffaire-ministerie-van-financien
114) https://www.ad.nl/binnenland/ambtenaren-belastingdienst-eisen-straf-voor-leid-ing~af9a295a/
115) https://www.trouw.nl/nieuws/discrimi-neert-de-belastingdienst-onderzoek-ge-start-naar-etnisch-profileren~b8c97834/
116) https://www.nu.nl/economie/6034123/belastingdienst-zette-mogeli-jke-fraudeurs-zonder-bewijs-op-zwarte-lijst.html
117) https://www.rijksoverheid.nl/regering/bewindspersonen/ferdinand-grapperhaus/documenten/kamerstukken/2020/02/18/tk-beantwoording-schriftelijke-vra-gen-ai-bij-de-politie
118) https://www.theguardian.com/technology/2019/jul/26/apple-contractors-regular-ly-hear-confidential-details-on-siri-recordings
119) https://www.rtlnieuws.nl/nieuws/nederland/artikel/5010961/syri-fraudedetector-fraudeopspor-ingssysteem-uitkeringsfraude
120) https://www.volkskrant.nl/nieuws-achter-grond/syri-het-fraudesysteem-van-de-overheid-faalt-nog-niet-een-fraudegeval-opgespoord~b-789bc3a/
121) https://www.nrc.nl/nieuws/2019/10/28/willen-we-dat-de-overheid-zo-met-burgers-omgaat-a3978217
122) https://pilpnjcm.nl/en/landslide-victory-in-syri-case-dutch-court-bans-risk-profiling/
123) https://www.amnesty.nl/mensenrech-ten-in-nederland/veiligheid-en-mensenrechten/sleepwet
124) https://www.grutjes.nl/2018/03/wiv-bouwen-we-onze-eigen-vernietigingsmachine/
125) https://nl.wikipedia.org/wiki/Wet_op_de_inli-chtingen-_en_veiligheidsdiensten_2017
126) https://www.bitsoffreedom.nl/2018/04/18/we-stappen-naar-de-rechter-om-de-sleepwet-aan-

te-vechten/
127) https://www.nrc.nl/nieuws/2018/01/23/
aivd-straks-gecontroleerd-door-oud-aivder-en-to-
padvocaat-a1589468
128) https://nos.nl/artikel/2262021-groot-risi-
co-dat-geheime-diensten-handelen-in-stri-
jd-met-nieuwe-wet.html
129) https://www.ctivd.nl/documenten/
persberichten/2019/02/06/index
130) https://nos.nl/artikel/2257428-kritiek-toezich-
thouder-op-uitvoering-inlichtingen-
wet-te-veel-is-onrechtmatig.html
131) https://nos.nl/artikel/2288579-aivd-en-mivd-
voldoen-nog-steeds-niet-aan-inlichtingenwet.html
132) https://www.ctivd.nl/actueel/
nieuws/2019/10/15/index
133) https://www.volkskrant.nl/nieuws-achter-
grond/aivd-ontevreden-over-nieuwe-toezichthoud-
er-die-oordeelt-over-tappen-hacken-en-afluister-
en~bb811c76/
134) https://www.nu.nl/tech/6015236/
commissie-inlichtingendiensten-voldoen-nog-alti-
jd-niet-aan-sleepwet.html
135) https://www.torproject.org/
136) https://www.ravage-webzine.nl/2018/02/24/
gevaren-van-sociale-media-surveillance/
137) https://www.nytimes.com/2020/01/18/
technology/clearview-privacy-facial-recognition.
html
138) https://www.buzzfeednews.com/article/
ryanmac/clearview-ai-fbi-ice-global-law-enforce-
ment
139) https://www.adformatie.nl/programmatic/
omzet-reclamebureaus-stijgt-met-15-procent-2018
140) https://www.grutjes.nl/2019/01/10yearchal-
lenge-de-machine-leert/
141) https://www.vox.com/policy-and-poli-
tics/2018/4/10/17222062/mark-zuckerberg-testi-
mony-graham-facebook-regulations
142) https://www.nrc.nl/nieuws/2018/05/22/
mark-zuckerberg-getuigt-voor-het-europees-parle-
ment-a1603790
143) https://tweakers.net/nieuws/163474/
ap-kreeg-27800-privacyklachten-in-2019-en-
slaakt-noodkreet-over-onderbezetting.html
144) https://www.forbrukerradet.no/undersokelse/
no-underseIsekategori/report-out-of-control/
145) https://fil.forbrukerradet.no/wp-content/
uploads/2020/01/2020-01-14-out-of-control-final-
version.pdf
146) https://vinotion.nl/nl/producten/
visense-crowddynamics/
147) https://nl.wikipedia.org/wiki/Deviant_gedrag
148) https://psycnet.apa.org/
record/2015-15154-006
149) https://www.tno.nl/nl/tno-insights/artikelen/
slimme-politiecamera-s-herkennen-straatgeweld/
150) https://www.cnbc.com/2018/03/17/facebook-
and-youtube-should-learn-from-microsoft-tay-rac-
ist-chatbot.html
151) Surveiller et punir: Naissance de la prison,

Michel Foucault 1975
152) https://www.grutjes.nl/2017/12/
nederlands-grootste-denker-over-integratie/
153) https://www.vpro.nl/programmas/
zomergasten/lees/gasten/2008/willem-schinkel.
html
154) https://www.cbs.nl/nl-nl/nieu-
ws/2003/03/489-gemeenten-in-2003
155) https://autoriteitpersoonsgegevens.nl/sites/
default/files/downloads/rapporten/rap_2003_
cameratoezicht.pdf
156) https://sargasso.nl/cameratoezicht-in-neder-
land-hoeveel-cameras-zijn-er-eigenlijk/
157) https://beveiligingnieuws.nl/nieuws/
statistieken/anderhalf-miljoen-bewakingscamer-
as-in-nederland
158) https://www.ed.nl/eindhoven/cameratoe-
zicht-stad-nog-niet-compleet~abddd537/
159) https://cursor.tue.nl/achtergrond/2018/
oktober/week-4/smokkelaars-en-vluchtelingen-op-
sporen-met-slimme-cameras/
160) https://www.heerlen.nl/gemeente-heerlen/
evaluatierapport-operatie-hartslag-(pdf).pdf
161) https://nl.wikipedia.org/wiki/Prostituant
162) https://autoriteitpersoonsgegevens.nl/nl/
nieuws/kentekens-niet-gebruiken-voor-identifi-
catie-van-prostituanten-%C2%A0
163) https://www.nu.nl/algemeen/200012/
hoerenlopers-mogen-niet-via-kentek-
en-worden-aangepakt.html
164) https://www.volkskrant.nl/nieuws-achter-
grond/identiteit-hoerenloper-blijft-geheim~-
b6e55ed9/
165) https://www.regioplan.nl/project/
cameratoezicht-in-de-openbare-ruimte/
166) https://www.bndestem.nl/overig/
sakkers-zat-verkeerd-met-aanbesteding-camera-
s~ad6f5274/
167) https://www.omroepbrabant.nl/
nieuws/39385/Sakkers-geen-commissaris-bij-VCS
168) https://www.nrc.nl/nieuws/2006/03/27/
burgemeester-onder-vuur-om-dure-order-
11103218-a824258
169) https://www.omroepbrabant.nl/
nieuws/39385/Sakkers-geen-commissaris-bij-VCS
170) https://www.omroepbrabant.nl/
nieuws/49788/Onrechtmatige-aanbesteding-Heer-
len-geen-fout-van-Sakkers
171) https://zoek.officielebekendmakingen.nl/
kst-28684-90-b1.pdf Evaluatie cameratoezicht nul-
meting, Regioplan, S. Dekkers 200
172) https://www.burgemeesters.nl/sites/www.
burgemeesters.nl/files/File/evaluatie
cameratoezicht Almere.pdf
173) https://www.vcsobservation.com/
vcs-observation/coppweb/
174) https://www.omroepflevoland.nl/
nieuws/70457/flevoland-chef-politiekorps-vertrekt
175) https://www.ad.nl/eindhoven/pastoor-wil-
geld-of-excuses-van-sakkers~a5301957/
176) https://www.ed.nl/eindhoven/sakkers-maat-

s-bijna-vol~a39d6e48/
177) https://hetccv.nl/onderwerpen/
hic-preventiewijzer/secure-lane/
178) https://hetccv.nl/fileadmin/Bestanden/
Onderwerpen/Database_overvalpreventie/
T08_2012_14-16_MV_Secure_lane.pdf
179) https://www.politie.nl/binaries/content/
assets/politie/algemeen/publicaties-archief/2012_
cba_ladingdiefstal_2008_2010.pdf
180) https://en.wikipedia.org/wiki/Crime_displace-
ment
181) https://zoek.officielebekendmakingen.nl/
blg-109722
182) https://zoek.officielebekendmakingen.nl/
blg-109722
183) Steeds meer beeld, evaluatie 5 jaar
cameratoezicht op openbare plaatsen
(Schrijenberg & Homburg 2010)
184) https://zoek.officielebekendmakingen.nl/
kst-28684-312.html
185) https://www.nrc.nl/nieuws/2010/11/18/
overal-moet-cameratoezicht-komen-ook-al-werkt-
het-11971113-a1351853
186) https://nos.nl/artikel/2278648-naamswijzig-
ing-ministeries-kost-32-miljoen-euro.html
187) https://www.rijksoverheid.nl/regering/
bewindspersonen/ferdinand-grapperhaus/
documenten/kamerstukken/2020/02/18/
tk-beantwoording-schriftelijke-vra-
gen-ai-bij-de-politie
188) https://www.universiteitleiden.nl/
nieuws/2019/07/artificiele-intelligen-
tie-en-ethiek-bij-de-nederlandse-politie
189) https://www.nu.nl/tech/6025903/
onduidelijk-hoe-vaak-gezichtsherkenning-bij-poli-
tie-leidt-tot-aanhoudingen.html
190) https://www.bitsoffreedom.nl/2019/10/30/
politie-feest-keihard-de-grens-over/
191) https://www.omroepbrabant.nl/
nieuws/218057/Prominente-politiecommissar-
is-uit-Eindhoven-geschorst-vanwege-corruptie
192) http://www.anti-corruptie.nl/politie
193) https://justitieenveiligheid.nl/criminee/
194) https://www.wodc.nl/binaries/1260-volledi-
ge-tekst_tcm28-68508.pdf
195) https://www.nrc.nl/nieuws/2019/03/05/
oud-politiecommissaris-gedaagd-wegens-val-
sheid-in-geschrifte-en-witwassen-a3908037
196) https://www.tue.nl/en/research/
research-institutes/top-research-groups/
intelligent-lighting-institute/infrastructure/
stratumseind/
197) https://www.linkedin.com/in/otto-vroe-
gop-73241440/
198) https://www.thehaguesecuritydelta.com/
about
199) https://docplayer.nl/43854038-Trillion-com-
munity-policing-op-stratumseind.html
200) https://uitspraken.rechtspraak.nl/
inziendocument?id=ECLI:NL:RBOVE:2019:2094
201) https://uitspraken.rechtspraak.nl/

inziendocument?id=ECLI:NL:RBOVE:2019:2095
202) https://youtu.be/s9dBAw_q5EU
203) https://youtu.be/tXk6TZ2jCqU
204) http://ruiter.cms.nederland.net/pagina/
kennisthemas/beveiliging/verslagsembev/index.
html
205) https://youtu.be/JD8Stp8ebsY
206) https://youtu.be/s9dBAw_q5EU
207) https://youtu.be/XXHTHYy_qql
208) http://www.criminee.nl/
209) http://rtr-nl.nl/index.php/news/74-keur-
merk-veilig-ondernemen-kvo
210) https://hetccv.nl/fileadmin/Bestanden/
Certificatie-en-Inspectie/Schema_s/Keurmerk_
Veilig_Ondernemen/kvo-english.pdf
211) https://www.ed.nl/eindhoven/
netwerk-van-hypermoderne-camera-s-op-stratum-
seind-in-eindhoven-gaat-politie-helpen~a1e8acee/
212) https://www.ed.nl/default/citybeacons-mak-
en-eindhoven-slimmer~a5e57ee7/
213) https://www.ed.nl/eindhoven/victoria-
park-in-eindhoven-wordt-living-lab~a0ab585e/
214) https://www.theguardian.com/cities/2018/
mar/01/smart-cities-data-privacy-eindhoven-utre-
cht
215) https://www.theguardian.com/
environment/2019/jun/04/latest-data-shows-
steep-rises-in-co2-for-seventh-year
216) https://nymag.com/intelligencer/2018/10/
un-says-climate-genocide-coming-but-its-worse-
than-that.html
217) https://www.nrc.nl/nieuws/2019/05/14/
datacenters-verbruiken-drie-keer-zoveel-stroom-
als-de-ns-a3960091
218) https://www.vn.nl/cameratoezicht-altijd-suc-
ces/
219) https://www.trouw.nl/nieuws/rapport-bewi-
jst-in-drie-gevallen-beinvloedde-ministe-
rie-van-justitie-het-wodc-onbehoorlijk~bb9e7128/
220) https://www.volkskrant.nl/nieuws-achter-
grond/wodc-verdwijnt-na-onderzoek-van-drie-
commissies-dan-toch-uit-de-toren-van-justitie~bf-
18faa7/
221) https://www.bitsoffreedom.nl/2014/12/16/
winnaars-big-brother-awards-opstellen-en-de-
nederlandse-scholen/
222) https://creativecommons.org/licenses/
by-sa/4.0/deed.nl
223) https://aisel.aisnet.org/ecis2019_rp/95/
224) https://research.tilburguniversity.edu/en/
publications/surveillance-privacy-and-pub-
lic-space-in-the-stratumseind-living-
225) https://creativecommons.org/licenses/by/2.0
226) https://www.forbes.com/sites/
niallmccarthy/2019/03/25/oil-and-gas-gi-
ants-spend-millions-lobbying-to-block-cli-
mate-change-policies-infographic/#21db64f77c4f
227) https://xkcd.com/2228/
228) https://creativecommons.org/licenses/
by-nc/2.5/
229) https://www.oxfam.org/sites/www.oxfam.

org/files/file_attachments/mb-extreme-carbon-inequality-021215-en.pdf

230) https://www.theguardian.com/environment/2019/sep/27/climate-crisis-6-million-people-join-latest-wave-of-worldwide-protests

231) https://www.theguardian.com/technology/2017/jan/04/anti-surveillance-clothing-facial-recognition-hyperface

232) https://www.businessinsider.nl/clothes-accessories-that-outsmart-facial-recognition-tech-2019-10/

233) https://www.grutjes.nl/2015/06/heeft-u-zich-een-hoedje-gespot/

234) https://www.wired.com/story/congress-facial-recognition-privacy-regulation/

235) https://www.perpetuallineup.org/

236) https://www.engadget.com/2020/02/11/european-commission-facial-recognition-guidelines/?guccounter=1

237) https://www.bright.nl/nieuws/artikel/5003481/toch-geen-europees-verbod-op-gezichtsherkenning-op-straat

238) https://theintercept.com/2020/02/21/eu-facial-recognition-database/

239) https://www.grutjes.nl/2017/10/dus-laat-me-even-samenvatten/

240) https://www.euractiv.com/section/data-protection/news/german-ministers-plan-to-expand-automatic-facial-recognition-meets-fierce-criticism/

241) https://youtu.be/ihKSHT7gIBY

242) https://twitter.com/patriotcoburn/status/1168006395884519425?s=21

243) https://www.theatlantic.com/technology/archive/2019/08/why-hong-kong-protesters-are-cutting-down-lampposts/597145/

244) https://www.theverge.com/2014/10/1/6877377/sophisticated-iphone-and-android-malware-is-spying-on-hong-kong

245) https://www.bbc.com/news/world-asia-china-48656471

246) https://twitter.com/JoshuaPotash/status/1192995877079715843

247) https://www.vpro.nl/programmas/door-het-hart-van-china/kijk/afleveringen/door-het-hart-van-china-7.html

248) https://www.privacynieuws.nl/databases/166-big-data/19785-china-rangschikt-alle-inwoners-wie-slecht-scoort-mag-trein-of-vliegtuig-niet-meer-op-en-dat-is-nog-maar-het-begin.html

249) https://www.nrc.nl/nieuws/2019/06/14/wij-hebben-u-in-de-gaten-a3963755

250) https://www.forbes.com/sites/zakdoffman/2019/07/02/chinas-latest-xinjiang-spying-smartphone-app-targets-tourists-instead-of-locals/#26adf542f90b

251) https://www.hln.be/nieuws/buitenland/human-rights-watch-trekt-aan-alarmbel-china-zet-big-data-in-om-burgers-preventief-op-te-pakken~aeb7d820/

252) https://www.dw.com/en/russian-court-rejects-call-to-ban-facial-recognition-technology/a-51135814

253) https://nos.nl/artikel/2294479-zorgen-om-chinese-camera-s-met-gezichtsherkenning-in-belgrado.html

254) https://www.telegraaf.nl/nieuws/1232956228/china-infiltreert-in-hart-van-europa

255) https://www.nu.nl/weekend/5936895/zo-zetten-overheden-gezichtsscanners-in-om-burgers-te-volgen.html

256) https://www.nytimes.com/interactive/2019/04/04/world/asia/xinjiang-china-surveillance-prison.html

257) https://www.nytimes.com/2019/04/14/technology/china-surveillance-artificial-intelligence-racial-profiling.html

258) https://techcrunch.com/2019/02/19/when-surveillance-meets-incompetence/

259) https://www.hikvision.com/europe/Partners/channel-partners/find-a-distributor/

260) https://ipvm.com/reports/hikvision-uyghur

261) https://nos.nl/nieuwsuur/artikel/2297468-omstreden-chinese-camera-s-in-de-ban-in-vs-hangen-nog-in-nederland.html

262) https://www.ajax.nl/streams/actueel/hikvision-europe-official-sponsor-ajax-1.htm

263) https://www.nytimes.com/2019/04/14/technology/china-surveillance-artificial-intelligence-racial-profiling.html

264) https://www.washingtonpost.com/opinions/2019/11/03/china-every-day-is-kristallnacht/

265) https://ipvm.com/reports/hikvision-uyghur

266) https://www.hartvannederland.nl/nieuws/2019/knvb-zet-slimme-cameras-om-racisme-stadions-te-bestrijden/

267) https://www.rtl.nl/nieuws/2019/11/29/dieven-en-onschuldigen-de-camera-ziet-iedereen-a3982154

268) https://qz.com/1599393/how-researchers-estimate-1-million-uyghurs-are-detained-in-xinjiang/

269) https://raadsinformatie.eindhoven.nl/user/bdocument/env=help/action=showannex/gdb=687/Bijlage_1_-_Nota_Digitalisering_van_de_stad.pdf

270) https://www.luciassociation.org/map-city/guangzhou/

271) https://chinatribunal.com/final-judgement-report/

272) https://www.independent.co.uk/news/world/asia/china-religious-ethnic-minorities-Uyghur-muslim-harvest-organs-un-human-rights-a9117911.html

273) https://www.ad.nl/politiek/blok-botst-met-kamer-over-mensenrechten-china~a6b637a9/

274) https://www.nzherald.co.nz/world/news/article.cfm?c_id=2&objectid=12295956

275) https://www.volkskrant.nl/nieuws-achtergrond/minister-dekker-moet-op-eieren-lopen-wil-hij-de-rechtsbijstand-nog-herzien~bcc68c99/

276) https://www.government.nl/government/
members-of-cabinet/sander-dekker/
news/2019/12/20/prohibition-of-anti-democrat-
ic-organisations-made-easier
277) https://www.rtlnieuws.nl/columns/
column/5050262/belastingdienst-toeslagenaf-
faire-zwarte-lijst
278) https://www.internetconsultatie.nl//wgs
279) https://twitter.com/pieterkleinrtl/
status/1237786601146679307
280) http://www.grutjes.nl/
281) https://www.sorama.eu/listener64
282) https://www.frogdesign.com/designmind/
evolution-of-a-smart-city-hub
283) https://www.rtlnieuws.nl/tech/
artikel/5168501/aivd-en-mivd-wilden-minder-vaak-
onterecht-hacken-en-afluisteren
284) https://www.nu.nl/binnenland/6061353/
aivd-zette-toezichthouder-op-ver-
keerde-been-door-verzwijgen-van-informatie.html
285) https://www.volkskrant.nl/kijkverder/v/2020/
de-stand-van-gezichtsherkenning-in-neder-
land~v91028/
286) https://autoriteitpersoonsgegevens.nl/nl/
nieuws/werkwijze-belastingdienst-stri-
jd-met-de-wet-en-discriminerend
287) https://www.rtlnieuws.nl/nieuws/
artikel/4763896/belastingdienst-men-
no-snel-tweede-kamer-toeslagen-ministe-
rie-van-financien
288) https://www.rtlnieuws.nl/nieuws/nederland/
artikel/5169750/belastingdienst-zwarte-li-
jsten-fraude-toeslagenaffaire
289) https://en.wikipedia.org/wiki/Human_rights_
in_Singapore

133

Notes

#1) The Dutch recently created a special minister for "Rechtsbescherming." Rechtsbescherming means legal protection, but not of databases against citizens, one would say. The Dutch word *rechtsbescherming* is slightly different from English and has the connotation of protecting citizens rights against for instance government. But Sander Dekker, the first minister of Legal Protection, doesn't seem to see it that way. He drastically cut access to legal aid, abolished parole,[275] and wants to make it easier for government to restrict fundamental rights on freedom of assembly and association.[276]

#2) Maurice de Hond is an influential Dutch opinion poller. He was convicted for libel in 2009, but continues to work. Critics point to his way of questioning, and to his results that consequently predict higher support for extreme right parties than other opinion pollers do.

#3) Many thanks to everyone who knowingly or unknowingly contributed to the many months of work on this long read. Including: Tammy Sheldon, Onomatopee, Rutger Schimmel, Bits of Freedom, Buro Jansen en Janssen, Vrijbit, Maša Galič, Øyvind Kaldestad and Forbrukerrådet Norway, Stefania Milan, Eva de Bruijn, Stichting Pandora, Wouter Engler, Tony Hisgett, xkcd, Sylvana Simons, Steve Hubback and Kat Arina, and of course Dr Who. Thank you!

Coronavirus and time

I wrote most of the above text before September 2019. As you probably noticed, English is not my native language. Spelling correction took much more time than any of us had ever anticipated. Especially after the first fast and thorough editor (Tammy Sheldon) had to quit because of a hectic job. (She was still helping me out while on a plane flying to NY to meet the UN secretary. I'm so proud to be able to call her my friend!) The second editor was not in such a hurry, migrated twice during the job, and then corona happened...

It's a pity. Many scoops in this article have been published by others many months after I wrote about this. Still, I hope you found the essay worth your while as it may give you an overview and a different take on what you will mostly encounter about these subjects. Also, there are still several scoops left that were not yet written about by anyone else.

I hoped this article would be a small bomb with enough impact to bring about some change. Now I'm cynical about that. And I won't hide the fact that I'm disappointed that this has taken so long.

I have added short pieces of text in the process, but nothing major since corona started. However, this is a different world we now live in, and I simply need to say something about it.

A new world — Or is it?

Since the pandemic, inequality has risen even more. Oxfam, January 2021: "The world's ten richest men have seen their combined wealth increase by half a trillion dollars since the pandemic began —more than enough to pay for a COVID-19 vaccine for everyone and to ensure no one is pushed into poverty by the pandemic. At the same time, the pandemic has ushered in the worst job crisis in over 90 years with hundreds of millions of people now underemployed or out of work." [1] Workers around the world lost \$3,7 trillion in the first year of the pandemic [2], billionaires made \$3,9 trillion. [3] Meanwhile, both in England and the Netherlands, poor people have twice the chance to die of Covid as rich people do. [4] The rich have been able to isolate themselves in luxury, working from home, while the poor were forced to go out and risk their health in factories, supermarkets, cleaning, order picking and deliveries.

CO_2 emissions plummeted at the beginning of the pandemic, but many governments, including the Netherlands, steered most of their Covid relief towards the fossil fuel industry and aviation. At this moment, Spring 2021, CO_2 emissions are already back to pre-corona levels and still rising.

There has been a high rise of extreme-right conspiracy theories, and the rise and normalisation of fascism have not been countered, despite the resignation of Trump.

When I wrote earlier in this article about the Uyghur situation, almost nobody knew about it in the Netherlands. This lack of knowledge has changed, and by now, most people have heard about the concentration camps. Yet, they don't seem to care. Earlier this week, I've seen and checked several Chinese human trafficking ads[5] selling Uyghur slavery labour and sex slavery, with a minimum batch of 50 workers per day. It didn't lead to upheaval. Although the Dutch parliament called the Chinese actions in Xinjiang "genocide", our government didn't change one bit in the Dutch-Chinese trade relationship. The EU had a minor diplomatic thingy but is still looking to expand a trade agreement with China.

Despite a few articles about Huawei [6] and other Chinese businesses involved in developing AI recognition of Uyghur for Chinese authorities, there has been very little attention. Huawei, like Hikvision before, is still engaged in Dutch smart city 'solutions', besides the genocide in China.

There's a new buzzword for their activities, which replaced the Living Labs: "FieldLab" football Arena and FieldLab Amsterdam Zuidoost.[7]

Social Darwinism and corona

Governments, especially in the 'free West', have chosen not to stop corona. Unlike countries like Bhutan, Vietnam, Niger or New Zealand, who (up until now) have a policy of zero Covid, nipping every minor outbreak in the bud, allowing them to open up society most of the time, and also have blooming economies and up until now virtually no deaths.

Instead, the European countries and the USA have opted for a semi-permanent lockdown. One that is not hard enough to suppress large scale corona infections, not enough to stop the dying, but enough of a lockdown to "mitigate": spread the dying over time, so healthcare is not overrun too much.

The Dutch prime minister initially opted openly for 'herd immunity', a strategy which was already proven lethal by me[8] and many others when he talked about it. Later on, he denied his own words and rephrased them as "maximum control", but it seems to still play a role in basic thinking.

The Dutch call their policy of infecting as many citizens as possible without over flooding the hospitals "sturen op de IC"—guided by the number of intensive care admissions. When the number is too low, the semi lockdown rules are relaxed; when the number is too high, schools and shops are closed again. This policy has led to at least 20.000 Dutch deaths in 2020 alone[9], around 1,5 million infections and probably about 150.000 cases of long Covid (as this is typically 10% [10]). These numbers are precisely the predictions[8] I made a year ago at the start of the first lockdown. Or the 'intelligent lockdown', as the chauvinistic Dutch call their policies, implying that everyone else is stupid.

Europe, the USA and a few other countries like Brazil are the biggest spreaders of the disease, and also the main breeding grounds for new mutations. Vaccines are developed, but mutations may develop even faster with this high level of infections, as every new infection creates the possibility of a new mutation.

Meanwhile, the EU and USA have prevented the free use of patents on vaccines. As a result, 75% of all vaccinations have been administered in 10 rich countries, while more than 130 countries have received none. (February 2021[11])

It seems the colonising countries think that colonisation, slavery and climate change were not yet enough to be ashamed of.

Social Darwinism—the idea that human rights are a hindrance, and human society benefits from sacrificing the weak to the survival of the fittest—has taken a strong foothold in Dutch society. Every week, a different group of people calls for 'freedom' and an end of the prevention measures; getting much media attention with slogans like 'dying is a normal part of life' [12], with which of course the death of the others, the 'weak' people, is meant.

Until now, Dutch media and politicians consider only two options viable: the semi-permanent lockdown or removing (almost) all prevention measures. In a strange cocktail of white superiority and victim playing, they refuse to learn from other countries. Masks were ridiculed, even by the RIVM, the national institute of health. The day the government made them mandatory, RIVM director Van Dissel told the media masks are 'not necessary' [13]) as if the feelings of white superiority will somehow protect us against what's called with condescension "Chinese / Italian / Brazilian style situations". But at the same time, the Dutch see themselves as helpless victims of circumstances. "We can't stop Covid here, as we're not an island like New Zealand." "We can't stop it because we're free, unlike China." And yes, I heard someone say, "we can't stop corona because we're not poor like Vietnam, and people want to buy things and go to shops and see each other".

The aforementioned Willem Schinkel calls the Dutch corona policies 'necro politics' [14]), which is not a conspiracy by some *cabal*, but pointing out the hegemony of neoliberal ideology. Politicians and media refuse to question the idea that we need to save big corporations before anything else. They consider health to be a personal responsibility. Not something the government is responsible for, but rather something we need to patronise workers about because they need to have a healthy lifestyle, so they keep being productive.

There's no real difference between the many political parties. During the latest elections in March 2021, corona was not one of the central debating points. A political ad about corona policies by the 'social-democratic' PvdA [15]), notably considered the most critical on corona policies of all parties currently in parliament, reads: "We need concrete plans to help people live healthier, eat healthily and exercise more". Nothing was said about any way to stop infections. In stead of that, people with health and immunity problems and people dying of Covid were shamed: they should have entertained a healthier lifestyle.

Most of these politicians are not mean on purpose, neither are the media that repeat them day and night without asking any real questions. It's not on purpose. They just don't see any alternative, even if all they need is to look to other countries like New

Zealand. They don't see it because their neoliberal ideology is blinding them. And it's not only politicians and media but also the people: although polls say most people support the preventive measures taken, only 40% stay at home when they are sick with corona. Despite this, most people think they uphold the rules, while others break them all the time.

What we've learned, also by example from a minister that broke the rules and then changed the rules so he wouldn't get a criminal record [16], is to think is that *restrictions apply to other people. Misery is not important to us, unless it's hitting us personally. The essential function of misery is not to solve it but to blame it on someone else, and solidarity is an unworldly idea that brought us Stalinism.*

Meanwhile, the cause of Covid, one could argue, is capitalism, as zoonotic diseases [17] have much more chance to surface in a system that thrives by urbanisation, exploiting nature, and constant global travelling.

So, what has all of this got to do with smart cities?
Neoliberal governments confuse problem-solving with surveillance. Instead of acting (a short but real lockdown to get the numbers manageable, then test-trace-isolate to get as close to 0 Covid as possible), the Dutch government seeks "maximum control". "Maximum control" means some 'temporal' preventive measures (masks, distance, closed shops) but also the state and city councils that monitor movements by the public, by 'anonymised' phone locations, by cameras and all the other tools in the box. Surveillance and policing by drones has been normalised [18] with corona as an excuse. The first tests with robot police dogs [19] are run now.

Protection of medical data has been lifted, without informing the public, with the introduction of the automatic 'Corona-opt-in': sharing all medical data between family doctors and hospitals, even when the patient in question has never agreed with that. [20]

139

Apart from a short eruption around the failed first introduction of the 'corona app', privacy concerns have been discarded. Although the *Autoriteit Persoonsgegevens*—the Dutch Authority of Data Protection—has assessed the corona app to be contrary to law, the government deployed it anyway.[21] They now want to add a "corona passport" that would give formerly infected people, vaccinated people, and (for a shorter validity period) tested people a free pass to forget about any preventive measures. Police and other surveillance personnel could ask to see your phone to check the app.

Screenshot of the government website on which the public could initially vote for the best corona app. Even the spelling was a disaster.

Instead of taking effective actions against corona, the curfew was prolonged so the barbers could open shop.[22] While every week large groups of 'Nazi-hippies' (new age and far-right corona conspiracy thinkers) demonstrate illegally (mostly unhindered for hours at a time, despite not keeping any distance from each other), anti-racist and climate activists face much repression. The latter can only come together with small groups, despite keeping distance and honouring preventive measures.[23]

Borders have been closed down worse than ever before to refugees, who are confronted with an immense rise in money for Frontex and anti-migration surveillance, and illegal pushbacks.[24]

Simultaneously a near stop of asylum procedures[25] locked asylum-seekers in the oubliettes we call refugee camps.

Meanwhile, both the Netherlands and the EU are heading for a ban on encryption for ordinary citizens—the government demands an open backdoor in all software. Once it's built, a back door can also be discovered and used by criminals and secret services other than the domestic ones.

Example: Palantir

Remember the Palantíri, those communication crystals in Lord of the Rings that enable you to watch everywhere? The crystals with which Sauron was able to corrupt Saruman the White?
The European Commission thinks we need that too.
The EU wants to build a European cloud service, called Gaia-X, which could be a good idea as the cloud services used by people and authorities now are primarily American. At the same time, we know that the US government happily taps into that cloud to hover up data. However, Gaia-X may become even worse, as the European Commission want Palantir to build it.[29]

Palantir Technologies was founded with money from the CIA, which is still a major investor. Peter Thiel, Palantir's founder and chairman, also is the founder of PayPal. Thiel is a billionaire that has supported Trump with millions and had many meetings with the extreme right. He's firmly opposing migration, although he's an immigrant himself. Shortly after dropping out of university, he wrote a book about how bad multicultural diversity, feminism and the left are supposed to be for education, downplaying the seriousness of rape in-between. He is openly anti-democratic: "I no longer believe that freedom and democracy are compatible." Thiel is a big player and a founder or investor in many of the companies we already talked about, for Instance, facial recognition firm Clearview AI.

His company Palantir tries to predict the future. Palantir is actively lobbying against any form of privacy. AI development and data mining of massive datasets are its primary activities. Palantir makes money out of data in anti-terrorism, predicting the stock market and predictive policing. It has a $91 million contract with the controversial ICE, the police agency that detains and deports migrants. Palantir helps ICE to round up and deport the parents of the children they put into cages. It does so by collecting and data mining everything about any citizen it can lay its hands on: data from street facial recognition cameras to telephone databases, financial data, to social media. But it's not only ICE to whom Palantir is "crucial". Palantir also works with the army and police of many countries, including NSA, CIA, and the US army (Palantir won an $800 million contract for building an intelligence system for the military) and France, Germany, Austria, Switzerland, Europol and the Netherlands.

Palantir worked with Cambridge Analytica and shared datasets with them. Palantir tried to stop Wikileaks with a disinformation campaign. Palantir is developing AI and pilotless drones in Project Maven, used for bombing and intelligence. Critics consider this the development of illegal autonomous weapons.

Amnesty International accuses Palantir of war crimes and mass human rights abuses in Syria[26], the US[27] and other countries. Bloomberg calls Palantir "a monstrous government snoop". New York Times: "particularly malignant avatar of the Big Data revolution". ACLU: "a totalitarian nightmare".

Palantir got access to Britain's healthcare data by offering their service for free at the beginning of the Covid pandemic to the NHS (Britain's healthcare system). December 2020, they were granted a secret 2-year contract that was only made public after being forced by lawsuits by Open Democracy. One clause says, "the services to be provided by Palantir extend to matters far beyond the response to the Covid-19 pandemic" -including Brexit, NHS workforce plans, and general government business.[28]

Palantir is the company that the European Commission wants to give all of our (pseudonymised) data. Like the Brits, the Commission name the pandemic as motivation to violate privacy and make haste and use Palantir instead of developing European solutions that do respect privacy.

A waterfall of infringements

Palantir is just one example—I don't have the time to tell about every massive infringement, as there are so many—the Dutch GGD, responsible for testing people for Covid, knowingly leaked everyone's data for a year.[30] The minister of healthcare wants to share every citizen's location data with RIVM (National Institute for Public Health) to combat Covid.[31]

Of course the Citybeacons are still standing in Eindhoven, and spreading into the world. As we've seen earlier, the *wethouder* told the city council that all sensors of these spying advertisement columns are shut down because of privacy regulations. As I showed, this is false. With the excuse of "tests", Citybeacons are deployed as data gathering tools for crowd control.
That was back in 2018. What has changed in the past three years? Not much. City marketing bureau Eindhoven247 thinks they don't have to hide the use of illegal spying on citizens any more. Their website now openly mentions the use Citybeacons for crowd control on big events, like the aforementioned Glow.[44] Other organizations see potential too. Consultant Stad&Co wants to deploy Citybeacons for crowd control and corona prevention.[45] NRIT Media happily advertises: "Collecting visitor data with Citybeacons in model country (sic) Eindhoven".[46] All of this is still contrary to the law.
Let's zoom out for some other infringements.

The Dutch professor Paul Abels researches "the supervision of the intelligence and security services and the ethics of intelligence gathering" at University Leiden.[32] He is known for his conservative and sometimes quite aggressive comments towards leftist academics on Twitter.[33] In his role of an independent scientist, he was one of the people that got a lot of visibility in the media, defending the WIV (or Sleepwet: The law that I wrote about before), which gives secret services the right to spy on large scores of people and even to hack their phones. Paul Abels published more than 60 articles and interviews, and was seen in major talk shows, telling people that the WIV was good for them and even good for privacy.

143

What many media failed to mention was that he is not an independent scientist at all. His professorship is paid for by the Dutch National Coordinator for Security and Counterterrorism (NCTV), which is part of the ministry of Justice and Safety.

Recently he was unmasked to the general public by newspaper NRC Handelsblad[34] as most important man (chief, later on senior advisor) of the data analytics department of NCTV. More importantly, the NCTV is illegally following citizens, politicians and activists on a large scale, with the use of fake social media accounts. Aggregated data are kept indefinitely. The resulting analysis prove to be of very low quality, with NCTV top figures that, according to NRC Handelsblad researchers, systematically downsize extreme right threats, and exaggerate the danger of Islam and especially Salafism.

The NCTV is not even meant to conduct investigations of their own, as they have a coordinating role within the ministry and are not an intelligence unit nor secret service. But when Abels was confronted with the upcoming article, he tried to threaten the journalists to prevent publication. The professor of Intelligence Ethics wrote to the journalists that it would "take [him] little effort" to discover the identity of the journalists' sources and start a "criminal investigation," saying that it would be wise to delete text "for [their] own safety."

There's so much more. The House of Representatives already approved the "Wet gegevensverwerking door samenwerkingsverbanden"—Data Processing by Partnerships Act—which basically makes sharing all data and AI data mining between every government service and commercial partners legal.[35] Only the Senate can stop it now, but it doesn't seem to want to do so. The best part of the law is that it does not say what data may be shared with whom: the minister can decide whatever he wants later, without consulting parliament.

Using Covid as an excuse and a false claim of growing violence against police, proven to be disinformation by police[36], a very similar law passed the House of Representatives providing tasers and rubber bullets to police. Moreover, when people die in police custody or by police violence, the law forbids to see police officers as a suspects in the initial investigation.[37)] Consequently, no evidence of criminal police violence is sought. If by miracle illegal and serious police violence is proven later, most evidence will be gone by then. Even then, police will be judged by a special court and can't be accused of more than one fact at a time, practically resulting in a maximum punishment of three years for murder.

Fun fact one: Only one month after almost every political party declared solidarity with the Black lives Matter movement, the House of Representatives unanimously agreed to the law except for the political parties Denk and Bij1. Fun fact two: Black Americans die in police custody 2.5 as frequently as white Americans. In the Netherlands, the numbers are very different: People with a non-Western migration background are *14 times* as likely to die in police custody as white Dutch people.[38)]

I could go on for pages, well actually a few books, if I wanted to.

The EU is not researching how to stop sharing personal data and AI decision-making but is exploring how to share not less but *more* data about citizens, even with commercial partners as "The availability of data is essential for training artificial intelligence systems". (European Commission: European data strategy[39)]).

Amnesty International concludes: "Covid led to a global attack on human rights".[40)]

Corona is the ultimate Shock Doctrine, Naomi Klein would say, but she would better herself and say the climate crisis is just beginning. The opportunities it poses to disaster capitalism are even more significant.

But let me just stop this insufferable list of dehumanisation.

Response

There is still some resistance—though not much. The Hong Kong movement is beaten down by Chinese repression. The social struggle in Chile continues, and was successful enough to get the tanks off the streets. China is continuing the genocide against Uyghur unhindered.

One can find tiny grains of hope in the tenacious and courageous resistance of people—in many cases, women—in Belarus, Poland, Kurdistan, Nigeria and Myanmar, and also in the Black Lives Matter movement around the globe.

Trump is out of office, but Trumpism has not disappeared.

Instead, extreme right conspiracy theories have eaten a big part of the resistance against a surveillance society. By stealing and perverting themes and slogans from the left, fascists are de-weaponising the radical left—or better: weaponising social struggle as a tool to promote fascism. For example, the Dutch extreme right *Viruswaarheid* movement weekly demonstrates against preventive corona measures that they compare to the Holocaust, claiming that Covid does not exist, calling the media "liars" and the health authorities "Nazis". They are declaring that they are 'fighting for love and the democratic rule of law, and against the fascist state', while at the same time their leader also says that "the extreme right is love" and actually wants to "end democracy".

It's becoming extra challenging to protest surveillance technology or even fascism without being seen as an extreme right "wappie"—a diminutive Dutch word for a conspiracy theorist. Meanwhile, fake news and gaslighting are not just weapons used by Alt-Right in the culture wars against the left. One could argue gaslighting is normalised as a political tool. Even by the government, both in deploying the failing Covid strategy[41] and in the complicated election crisis[42] that followed out of the evaluation of the 'Toeslagenwet'—the racist AI profiling by tax authorities we wrote about earlier, and that forced the fall of cabinet Rutte III.

Meanwhile, news media, especially Dutch media, fail hopelessly as a watchdog of democracy. They discovered that hate, fear and upheaval sell much more papers than sex ever did. Every prominent Dutch newspaper has at least one far-right columnist on the payroll. TV talk shows are even worse. As Léonie de Jonge (PhD) concluded after years of research: Dutch media and especially talk shows have facilitated the rise of the far-right by giving far-right politicians "disproportionate attention" that lacked any criticism. By not confronting them with their racist and antisemitic statements and giving them a place at the table, talk shows are actually 'normalizing' those views and politicians. The difference in news-media approach and the corresponding number of far-right seats in parliament between the Netherlands and Wallonia is telling.[43]

On the other hand, investigative journalism, substantive critics in a talk show, and any media giving attention to, for example, smart cities' downsides are very rare.

In the Netherlands, despite the reputation of being tolerant, progressive and frank—well, blunt—discussing vital principles or even entertaining a political view that is more fundamental than "I like this kind of cheese better" is frowned upon. Talk shows deal in clickbait, gossip and pundits, not in visions or fundamental criticism. Compared to the Anglo-Saxon world, public discussion is barely existing. Maybe we already knew that, but the pandemic and the lack of fundamental discussion about it in the Netherlands has made it all the more evident. And this is devastating to guarding human rights and protecting privacy from surveillance capitalism.

How to conclude this lamentation?

The world is clearly at a breaking point. In the past 'social contract' (as proponents called it), the working class supported the upper class in exchange for a small piece of the pie: a car, a holiday, slow increase of wealth. (And besides that, the exploitation of the working class was, of course, also enforced by divide and conquer. By creating a *lower* class of people of colour and women, for the working class to feel superior through racism and sexism.)

But this model has reached its limits. Exponential, eternal growth is just not possible any more. Virtually every market is already served, so it's becoming increasingly difficult to generate growing profits. And the climate- and environmental crisis is spelling an end to exploiting nature as well.

When spreading tiny bits of prosperity to the working class, or even just the middle class, is not profitable any more, and not even possible without giving up huge profits for the few, the social contract is broken.

When there's nothing left to eat, but you still want to eat more and more and more, there's just one solution: eat your own.

That is the new phase of capitalism. Neoliberalism already started eating the welfare state in the eighties. Trumpism finishes the job by eating the state itself, and after that having a dessert by consuming faltering democracy and human rights.

The system discovered you don't need to appease people with growing prosperity. You can also enslave them into debt. No prosperity required; on the contrary: Precarisation of people is key in the gig economy by making their jobs flexible, their healthcare and pensions, their homes and their precarious lives. People that are made insecure about everything will not protest. They need all their mental and physical energy just to survive. You can exploit them without giving anything in return.

Surveillance capitalism is the cornerstone of this new phase of capitalism. The technocrats feel safe: whether the centre-left—that now holds views we would have called hard right 25 years ago—comes to power, or the fascists will. Both will need their solutions, as neither one wants a radical alternative (or even considers the possibility) for this final capitalist phase.

That is what's happening. It's not a conspiracy by a secret world government that eats your babies, as the QAnon creeps claim. It's just a business opportunity.

All in all, the pandemic could have triggered a clean break with the capitalism that caused it. Instead, it reinforced it all.
Unless we act[47], it will keep that way, exponentially so.
It's up to you if you let them.

It's up to you if you want to wallow in cynicism, "there's no alternative", and let them extinguish your spark of life in exploited lethargy in a Panopticon run by the likes of Peter Thiel. Or if you rather want your little one-time-only spark to bloom and blaze in the social fight, and claim not just your square millimetre and your right to exist, but ours, together.

Yes, I'm saying that not just to you, but to myself as well.

Bas Grutjes

With many thanks to Heidi Dorudi (yes, editor number 3) for correcting my Dunglish.

Sources

1) https://www.oxfam.org/en/press-releases/mega-rich-recoup-covid-losses-record-time-yet-billions-will-live-poverty-least
2) https://www.businessinsider.com/workers-lost-37-trillion-in-earnings-during-the-pandemic-2021-1
3) https://www.businessinsider.com/billionaires-made-39-trillion-during-the-pandemic-coronavirus-vaccines-2021-1
4) https://www.volkskrant.nl/nieuws-achtergrond/gezondheidskloof-nog-duidelijker-door-corona-arm-sterft-twee-keer-zo-vaak-als-rijk~b9bc978ba/
5) https://twitter.com/GrauweGrutjes/status/1371496178655891457
6) https://tweakers.net/nieuws/175730/huawei-werkte-mee-aan-vler-surveillancesystemen-met-etniciteitherkenning.html
7) https://www.johancruijffarena.nl/over-ons/innovatie/
8) https://www.grutjes.nl/2020/03/covid-19-stoppen-of-afremmen/
9) https://www.nu.nl/coronavirus/6126242/meer-dan-20000-mensen-overleden-vorig-jaar-aan-gevolgen-coronavirus.html
10) https://twitter.com/MarionKoopmans/status/1365585994070831108
11) https://edition.cnn.com/2021/02/18/world/united-nations-130-countries-no-vaccine-trnd/index.html
12) https://www.scienceguide.nl/2020/03/we-moeten-accepteren-dat-het-risico-van-de-dood-bij-het-leven-hoort/
13) https://www.trouw.nl/binnenland/mondkapjes-per-1-december-verplicht-in-publieke-binnenruimtes-maar-de-discussie-gaat-door~b55b6eb9/
14) https://decorrespondent.nl/12188/welkom-in-de-eeuw-van-de-necropolitiek-waar-bedrijven-en-staat-over-lijken-gaan/859165661376-5b62f7fb
15) https://www.facebook.com/lilianne.ploumen/posts/4000381236674004
16) https://www.parool.nl/nederland/grapperhaus-bruiloftsblunder-heeft-niets-te-maken-met-lagere-coronastraf~bb435bde/
17) https://theconversation.com/global-urbanization-created-the-conditions-for-the-current-coronavirus-pandemic-137738
18) https://www.omroepgelderland.nl/nieuws/2446874/Drone-ingezet-om-te-controleren-of-mensen-zich-aan-coronaregels-houden
19) https://www.omroepbrabant.nl/nieuws/3354976/uniek-beeld-politie-gebruikt-speciale-robothond-na-explosie-in-drugslab
20) https://www.knmg.nl/actualiteit-opinie/nieuws/nieuwsbericht-corona/betere-gegevensuitwisseling-in-de-strijd-tegen-corona.htm
21) https://autoriteitpersoonsgegevens.nl/nl/nieuws/ap-privacy-gebruikers-corona-app-nog-onvoldoende-gewaarborgd
22) https://nos.nl/artikel/2369689-avondklok-3-weken-langer-scholen-deels-open-kappers-mogen-aan-de-slag.html

23) https://www.greenpeace.org/static/
planet4-netherlands-stateless/2021/03/3aa818fe-2
10305-brief-klimaatalarm-en-recht-op-protest.pdf
24) https://www.trouw.nl/buitenland/
het-ene-na-het-andere-schandaal-wie-controleert-
eu-grensbewaker-frontex~bd98a076/
25) https://www.raadvanstate.nl/@123681/
coronavirus-overmacht-asielprocedures/
26) https://www.amnesty.org/download/
Documents/MDE2413702015ENGLISH.PDF
27) https://www.amnesty.org.uk/press-releases/
usa-concerns-over-tech-giant-palantir-involve-
ment-immigration-enforcement
28) https://www.bbc.com/news/technol-
ogy-56590249
29) https://www.volkskrant.nl/nieuws-achter-
grond/dit-is-het-controversiele-amerikaanse-da-
tabedrijf-dat-europa-s-eigen-clouddienst-wil-
helpen-bouwen~be41af45/
30) https://www.rtlnieuws.nl/tech/artikel/5211164/
ggd-corona-systemen-toegang-vog-coronit-hp-
zone-light
31) https://www.rtlnieuws.nl/tech/
artikel/5190458/telecomdata-rivm-locatiege-
gevens-experts-tweede-kamer
32) https://web.archive.org/web/20201101014827/
https://www.universiteitleiden.nl/medewerkers/
paul-abels
33) https://twitter.com/NadiaBouras/
status/1380836849615183880
34) https://www.nrc.nl/nieuws/2021/04/09/
onmin-en-uitglijders-bij-de-club-die-het-land-
moet-beschermen-a4039114
35) https://www.nysingh.nl/blog/wet-ge-
gevensverwerking-samenwerkingsverbanden-wgs/
36) https://www.vpro.nl/argos/lees/onderwerpen/
artikelen/2020/stroomstootwapen-nieuws.html
37) https://www.grutjes.nl/2020/06/
blacklivesmatter-nl-politici-maken-poli-
tiegeweld-straffeloos/
38) https://www.opendemocracy.net/en/
oureconomy/we-shouldnt-be-surprised-by-the-
chaos-in-the-netherlands/
39) https://ec.europa.eu/info/strategy/
priorities-2019-2024/europe-fit-digital-age/
european-data-strategy_en
40) https://www.amnesty.nl/actueel/
jaarboek-amnesty-international-coro-
na-leidt-wereldwijd-tot-aanval-op-mensenrechten
41) https://www.containmentnu.nl/articles/
dossier-herd-immunity-in-the-netherlands
42) https://www.grutjes.nl/2021/04/
motie-van-lafkeuring/
43) https://www.nrc.nl/nieuws/2021/03/18/
als-je-schaarste-creeert-wil-iedereen-je-heb-
ben-a4036398
44) https://www.eindhoven247.nl/nl/projecten/
ondersteuning-glow-eindhoven
45) https://stadenco.nl/projectstad/
actieplan-de-nieuwe-binnenstad-eindhoven/
46) https://www.nritmedia.nl/kennisbank/40870/
Bezoekersdata_verzamelen_met_Citybeacons/
47) https://theintercept.com/2020/10/01/
naomi-klein-message-from-future-covid/

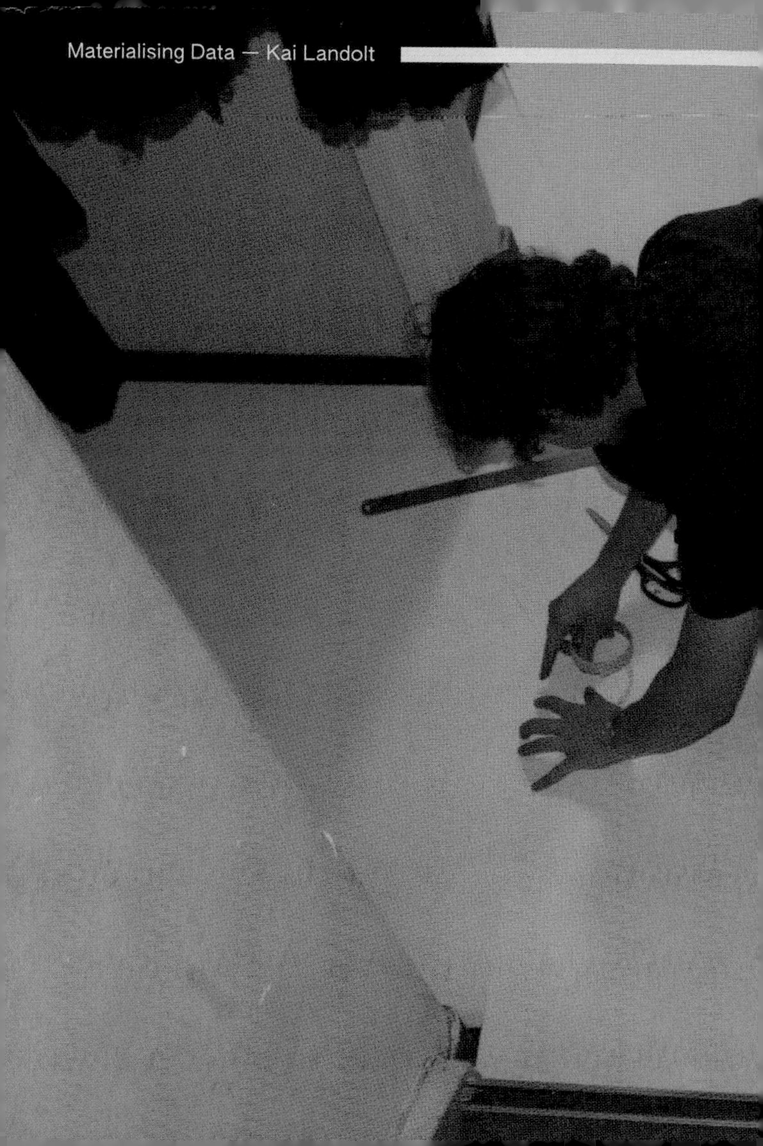

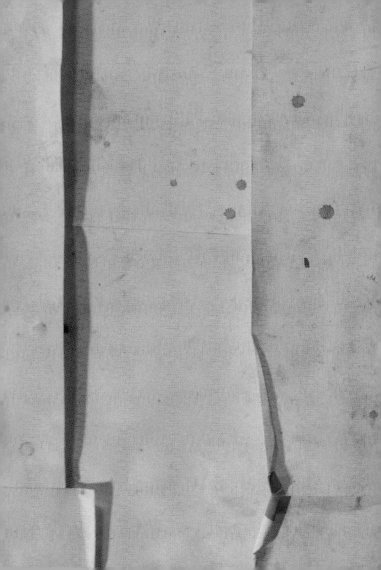

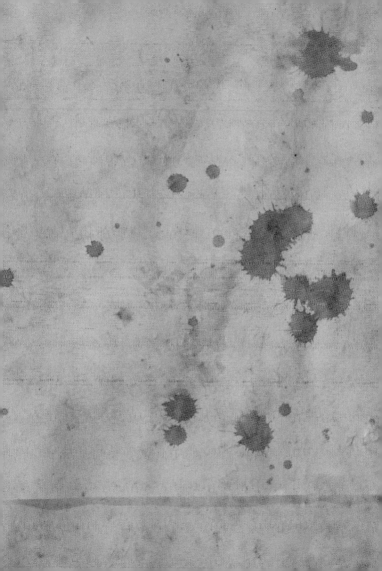

A raw and physical documentation of human
existence in a shared living environment.
Made using paper to obtain and record the reality
of a student house.

The Tale

Sjamme
van de Voort

(C)overt Knowledge Production in the City:

Where Truth Spots are Concealed, Spaces of Knowledge Production equal Control

> *It was the best of times, it was the worst of times, it was the age of wisdom,*
> *it was the age of foolishness, it was the epoch of belief, it was the epoch of incredulity, it was the season of Light, it was the season of Darkness, it was the spring of hope, it was the winter of despair, we had everything before us, we had nothing before us, we were all going direct to Heaven, we were all going direct the other way—in short, the period was so far like the present period, that some of its noisiest authorities insisted on its being received, for good or for evil, in the superlative degree of comparison only.*
> (Charles Dickens, A Tale of Two Cities)

Although the above quote plunges me headfirst into a realm where cliches are hard to avoid, I cannot escape its relevance. Systems of incomprehensible scale are understood best when viewed from their more than one vantage point – and especially the extremes. The development, employment and consequences of tools of mass-surveillance is just such a system.

On one end of this system, we find ourselves in Eindhoven, the Netherlands. Here we can listen to considerations from citizens concerned with data protection, noticing that the urban environments of Stratumseind and Strijp-S in Eindhoven are being rigged with wifi-trackers, cameras and microphones able to detect aggressive behaviour. These initiatives are part of the Triangulum Project, a framework set up to demonstrate, disseminate and rep-

176

licate solutions and frameworks for Europe's future smart cities. This end of the system is also where we hear the CEO and founder of Sorama, the company producing the microphones that track movement in this new cityscape, promising that their systems will not be sold to unsavoury parties such as the Chinese government. On this end of the system, there is apparently nothing to worry about: laws regarding privacy exist and are not broken, citizens can voice concerns through democratic processes and even the leader of the developers behind the technology seems to have good intentions.

On the other end of the system, we find ourselves in Tianjin, China, a city on the periphery of the Triangulum Project. Whereas the other cities in the project (Manchester UK, Eindhoven NL, Stavanger NO, Leipzig D, Prague CZ and Sabadell ES) are situated solidly in a legal and socio-cultural framework that – on paper, at least – seems to take privacy into consideration, Tianjin is not. The Liberal Democracy Index, published by the Varieties of Democracy Project, using the largest collection of data points on issues related to democracy, China holds a position in the bottom of the chart as number 169 of 179, while Norway, the Netherlands, the UK, Germany and the Czech Republic hold numbers 1, 9, 12, 17 and 36, respectively. This puts China in the category of a 'closed autocracy' and demands that we look at it through a different lens. The city council of Tianjin is not elected, surveillance is official policy as the national Cybersecurity Law requires internet companies to censor users' content and Tianjin is the home to the censorship hub of the largest Chinese microblogging network, Heibo.

To put it more simply, closed autocracies – dictatorships – do not play by the rules that give Sorama the confidence to promise that their technology will not be used for nefarious purposes. The Chinese government does not have to worry about upcoming elections, it has all sectors of the state at its disposal to further its goals and it does not care about promises made by CEOs in the Netherlands. To believe that a state with vast cyber-divisions, both capable and willing to covertly appropriate intellectual property and which has been perfecting the art of surveillance since its foundation, is either naive or delusional. Even if we are kind enough to assume the former, it seems like the road to mass-surveillance on one end of the spectrum is paved with the good intentions of the developers on the other end.

A radical answer to this dilemma would be to suggest a boycott of states conducting mass surveillance from programmes such as the Triangulum Project, although this answer would be informed by a false morality, given that we know that these actors will get their hands on this technology through their covert efforts anyway. An even more radical answer would be to suggest that we simply do not promote the further development of these technologies, although this answer borders on the ridiculous, given that this in its extreme would mean the end of free knowledge production. Let us instead of jumping to radical conclusions dwell on this key dynamic and goal of the system: knowledge production in the city. Whereas James Bond's Aston Martin and the NSA's data harvesting technologies are developed in the secret laboratories of Q-Branch and Fort Meade, the knowledge that will likely form the basis of surveillance in Tianjin is developed in the streets of Eindhoven, in the relatively open and free society of the Netherlands. This means that we find ourselves in an incredible position, where we on our end of the spectrum can actually have a conversation about the development of technology that will serve as surveillance tools on the other.

In order to have this conversation, I will first step back and make a couple of important assumptions to be able to talk about how knowledge is produced, fluctuated and kept within the system. First, knowledge does not exist in a vacuum but arises out of a context. It is a selection of memories based on certain principles such as the degree of truth that they hold and what importance they have to our life. Sociologist Maurice Halbwachs, famous for his contributions on the sociology of knowledge, wrote that: "No memory is possible outside frameworks used by people living in society to determine and retrieve their recollections." In a group of friends, it is not possible to remember that one funny incident that happened at that one get-together, without the sociological framework of the group to remind us. In a society, it is not possible to remember that one particular battle fought by that one famous king, 500 years ago, without the historiographical framework of the country to remind us.

The city, too, is such a framework. The network of streets, the buildings and spaces between them determine the movement and the activities that are possible within the realm of the city and by walking the streets, recognising the buildings, moving and acting, we exercise those memories everyday. Using a double dichotomy, cultural theorist Aleida Assmann has divided the exercises of memory into four possible categories: actively or passively remembering or forgetting. We can rehash that funny incident in our group of friends, committing it to active remembering, we can try to avoid it, committing it to the grey area of passive remembering and passive forgetting, or we can decide never to mention it again, committing it to active forgetting, taboo and censorship. These four possible exercises go beyond the collective memory that takes place in the social processes of a group of friends and repeat themselves in the choosing of which stories we select for our history books, which literature we put on a curriculum, which art we put in a gallery. The active remembering in these fixed structures is what is called a canon. Compared to the fluctuating sociological dynamic in a group of friends and even the writing of history, the city is solid, set in stone, and therefore perhaps the most fixed of canons.

Canon, it goes beyond saying, is a place from which power flows. The social dynamic in that one group of friends will decide who is the butt of the joke and history will be written by the victors. The city is subject to the same dynamic. Memories of Paris are held by the Eiffel Tower, the Louvre and Notre Dame and whereas a fire in the latter makes international headlines, a fire in the Banlieue will hardly be noticed beyond the arrondisement. The knowledge stored in some places in the city is worth more than others. Thomas Gieryn has called these places of exalted value within the canon of knowledge production 'truth spots'.

Could any place be a truth-spot? A gringo bartender who serves up trendy mezcal, recalling his visit to a tiny village distillery in out-of-the-way Oaxaca, told sociologist Sarah Bowen: "I was outside, under a steel shack—you know, two fermentation tanks, not even tanks, wooden tubs. And I'm [thinking]: this is the truth ... This is the truth." In a business where authentic and exotic stuff carries a premium, finding and experiencing the place where small-batch mezcal was made the old-fashioned way affirmed its value, its integrity, its reality—not so different from rounding Mount Parnassus and getting that first glimpse of the oracle site at Delphi, or finally reaching the end of the pilgrimage to Santiago de Compostela. The truth, it seems, is where you find it.

A place in Gieryn's terminology consists of three elements. Firstly, there must be a unique location in geographic space. Secondly, a place consists of material stuff gathered at this spot, both natural and human-made, objects and geological features made or found there that give the place a solid physicality and finally, a place contains narrations, interpretations, and imaginations that give the place distinctive meaning and value. If these three elements are present, a place has the ability to perform certain actions. Places manipulate time. Western tourists coming home from Havana, Cuba, tell tales of having visited a place stuck in time, while the same people coming home from a visit to Tokyo would tell stories of futuristic science fiction. Places gather together or separate, impose order or remain messy, expose or hide to control narrative and finally, they are either unique or standardised.

The aim of the Triangulum Project is to harvest the truths produced in its partner cities and use it to build a 'smart city' – that is, a city that uses available data to promote objectively decent goals: efficiency, noise control, crime prevention, safety. By framing spaces that gather narratives, exposing them to analysis, they create a standardised practice for canonization. The name that the project has given these spaces, the Living Lab, even reflects the truth-spot par excellence, the laboratory. As mentioned further above, the problem is not whether we need laboratories; off course we do. The problem is rather the power generated by control over the canon.

On the Eindhoven end of the spectrum, power over the canon, as well as power generated by the canon, is technically relegated to and by its civilian government bodies. It was the municipality of Eindhoven that took the initiative to establish the Living Lab, although it shares the stakes with private sector institutions and business interests. In policy briefs on digitalisation strategy from the Eindhoven municipal council, we can read about the intention to include citizens in the development process through 'user participation'. This is done through events at the Dutch Technology Week as well as the Dutch Design Week, open to the public. It is notable that the policy briefs sideline 'collaboration with citizens', with 'collaboration with businesses' and 'collaboration with other government agencies'. This means that collaboration with citizens in the formation of the canon is scaled down to be a 'collaboration with citizens that show up to specific professional events' and that the business sector, interested in growth of capital, and the state sector, interested in growth of control, are effectively in charge of the design of these truth-spots. The ideological dimensions of this skewed balance of power are enormous.

The obfuscation of the implementation process in Eindhoven notwithstanding, there is no comparison to the skewed power balance on the other end of the spectrum, where the government of Tianjin is selected by Communist Party officials and where business and state interests are one and the same. The difference between the two requires naming. One end could be called liberal democratic and the other closed autocratic, one end free and the other dictatorial, and the means of control these systems employ on one end open to civilian scrutiny, overt, and the other closed, covert. What I am doing here is not painting a tale of doom and gloom to come, I am not predicting a move of autocratic practices from one end of the spectrum to the other, nor am I suggesting the halt of technological development for the improvement of future democratic cities. What I am doing is rather to suggest that we see the spectrum for what it is: a system through which knowledge is developed in a liberal democracy that will inform the surveillance practices in a closed autocracy, but also a system through which we can glance into these practices and gain insights that could and should help us to design models of understanding.

Aleida Assmann's model for understanding the actions that steer collective memory is a good starting point for such a design. The double dichotomy, active and passive, remembering and forgetting, is however not sufficient to understand the difference between the two ends of the spectrum that we are trying to explain here. On both ends, memories created by citizens in their urban spaces are used actively to guide a response from the masters of the canon and then stored passively in databases. This means that similar mixtures of active and passive remembering are taking place on both ends of the spectrum. To capture the differences generated by the system set in motion by the Triangulum Project, we need to add the dichotomy overt-covert to Assmann's model. It is quite easy to understand the covert aspect of the active remembering model in the system of mass surveillance in China that the Triangulum Project risks enhancing. It is a system that is completely closed off to public scrutiny, run by a state security apparatus whose main interest is control over the citizenry to protect the autocratic government in power. It is a system that Soroma, having already assured us, is not in any way interested in aiding and abetting. Similarly, the council of the city of Eindhoven promises to collect, keep and use the data harvested through the project abiding the ethics guidelines set forth by the Data Ethics Decision Aid (DEDA), developed by the Data School at the University of Utrecht. Finally, the city council of Eindhoven is a democratically elected body, which means that oversight is fundamentally relegated to the citizenry. The addition of the overt-covert dichotomy to Aleida Assmann's model does, however, mean that it is now up to the citizenry to determine just how overt this process is.

As an entirely new spatiality of a truth-spot is developed, it must commit to be actively overt, fully transparent, for it not to contribute to the creation of a canon that centralises power beyond democratic control. The latter would turn citizens in the City as a Living Lab into lab rats navigating the labyrinth set up by lab technicians. A democratically designed truth-spot would dress Eindhoven citizens in lab-coats and give them the instruments they need to participate in the 'Living Lab'. This would give them the agency to not only influence their own truths in their own city but also understand the full spectrum of the knowledge flow that connects this tale of two cities.

We form a circle with each
person facing another.

We take out our smartphones
from our pockets and
aim them at the person
opposite.

We take three photos:
one crouching,
one standing normally,
one with our arm outstretched as high as possible.

We collect the images and
using open-source
photogrammetry software
we kit them
together.

Our moment of togetherness is
reconstructed in the virtual world.

The Account

Helen Milne

Eindhoven: Residency, Protest & Digital Presence

Criticism in the city can mean many things, but here it provides a platform for understanding the conflicted relationship between the digital image and lived experience of residency in Eindhoven. It was during one of our weekly meetings that these words popped up: 'Research can exist in a space so long as it inhabits it. And just being present, does not equate to presence.' This text explores the connection between inhabitancy, protest and digital presence. Like all major cities in The Netherlands, Eindhoven residents face a severe lack of housing: what differs is the representation of the issue. Eindhoven has seen exponential growth in population over the past few years; as a result of both company and university expansion, but its residents don't shout as loud about the issue as those in other cities like Amsterdam or Rotterdam. It was only in late 2018, when the city reached a tipping point, that the Gemeente (Municipality) openly addressed the issue for the first time. How does this relate to the 'digital image' of a technocratic city? The desire for 'frictionless' living is evident here.

The Dutch government requires every citizen who plans to stay in The Netherlands for longer than 4 months to register at their local municipality - understandable. However in order to register, and to be awarded the holy grail of residence – a Burgerservicenummer (BSN) - you must have an address, which is a luxury in a city that doesn't have enough available housing for its hopeful residents. A BSN is required for official online digital interactions, and some physical interactions with the city itself: the digital image and lived experience collide on a regular basis. Basic Dutch health insurance, which is mandatory for all who wish to work in the country, a Dutch bank account, the right to vote, reduced rate travel on public transport and disposal of waste are only available to those with a BSN. The reliance on this automated and seamless system is an extreme oversight for a country that continually runs into crises over housing. Municipalities do not keep up with their projected goals and image: funding in Eindhoven is allocated to developing technology innovation, but not to housing solutions (temporary or otherwise). The city undermines itself.

A web of QR codes and officially headed emails cannot tame the chaotic nature of real life, and yet the future citizens of Eindhoven only quietly vent their frustrations on Facebook housing groups: have the residents of this city become so used to smooth, frictionless living that they just accept that this is the way it will be? We Want Woonruimte Eindhoven (WWWE), a grassroots organisation that 'hopes to unite, understand, and catch public attention surrounding the topic of student housing in Eindhoven and the Netherlands' says otherwise. On 27th October 2018, during Dutch Design Week, We Want Woonruimte Eindhoven organised a protest: 'The Struggle Is Real: Protest for Student Housing, Eindhoven'.

Situated in the commercial epicentre of Dutch Design Week, Strijp-S, this protest could be seen as research inhabiting a space. In a city that lacks urgency and disruption, the success and outcomes of this action were unknowable. Eindhoven's main focus currently is on the expansion and positive image of the city. As part of this, the redevelopment of Stratum (a costly procedure, which includes removing the already acceptable red paving bricks), takes priority over building housing for its residents.

Being present to create 'presence' here was necessary: creating and manifesting an analogue event incites the tension and energy created by collective action. This potential energy is feared, particularly by institutions with a brand image to keep intact. We Want Woonruimte Eindhoven's call to action was mainly communicated and disseminated by a Facebook event. So much can (and has been) said about this; but in this case, it should be embraced when used for grassroots political action. It is a more economic and faster option than printing flyers and posters, and travels way beyond the geographical location of the protest. Once legalities are sorted, a call to action can be written and posted in minutes; and has the all-important 'attending' or 'interested' button. This creates a digital manifestation of that same disruptive energy of a group of individuals gathered in a space – the act of signalling interest in an event is an act of solidarity, similar to signing a petition.

Through initial connections made at Eindhoven Footnotes to individuals in the city, a web greater than any technology can provide - one of human connection, breakfast meetings, radio shows and phone books, was created - and enabled the potential audience of the protest to grow. Footnotes & Onomatopee, Siem Nozza (Nachtburgermeester), Eva De Bruijn and RaRaRadio, all backed this initial protest digitally and certainly played a part in the dissemination of the message. Whether or not the people who clicked 'interested' or 'attending' showed up on the day is not relevant; when successful it creates an intimidating digital presence that hints at disruption, and caught the attention of many significant parties. This concept of intimidating digital presence for grassroots political action is something that needs to be explored more. Organising physical protests is now just one part of a larger action in our digital culture. Particularly in smaller cities like Eindhoven that lag behind others in terms of facilitating applications and self-organised protests, these numbers created by online events are gaining legitimacy. In a city governed by stakeholders, that falls short of successful data collection and synthesis, raw data needs to be created, collected and delivered. Without any need for privacy invasion or data breaches, WWWE harnessed dissatisfaction in numbers – numbers the Gemeente so desperately need. The scale of the housing issue in Eindhoven is not fully known because there is no system in place to record the people who cannot register. This closed loop needs to be broken and a culture of transparency initiated. Grassroots initiatives like Eindhoven Footnotes and We Want Woonruimte go someway to making this happen. By researching, creating presence and demanding meetings with the Gemeente, as well as participating in the initiation of a bestuurgroep and a huurteam, the conversation across the city is widened to include a multitude of voices.

The Struggle Is Real: Protest for Student Housing, Eindhoven

Wij nodigen je uit. Studenten zonder huis, onderwoners, mensen die de status-quo willen opschudden. Ondersteun ons in protest tegen de (studenten) woning nood in Eindhoven.

Zaterdag 27.10.18
12.00 - 17.00
Verzamelen Ketelhuisplein
(Strijp-S)

The Struggle Is Real: Protest for Student Housing Eindhoven
Hosted by We Want Woonruimte

Lichellgence
Intelligence was not invented by us,
it was around long before.

The word Lichelligence is used here to describe the complex processes and ability to perceive information and retain it as knowledge to be used towards adaptive behaviours within an environment. It's a driving force behind evolution through learning, comprehension, self-awareness, compromise, logic, calculation, creativity and problem solving. Our usual reaction to intelligence it to imagine that it requires a brain like ours – the peak of evolution. Every innovation we create is in order to replace, extend or augment our bodily functions. We therefore end up constructing a system based on our own experiences. Take a computer, something based on a processor that almost acts like a brain, which controls all the hard and software connected to it. We are transferring our organs to an artificial intelligence with the same organic and animalistic architecture as our own. Even our societies are organised with this archaic, hierarchical and centralised system. But is this the most suitable approach to our contemporary conditions?

Through billions of years on earth other forms of intelligence have developed. However they've extended Into a completely different direction to our own. Where we as humans count on centralised and hierarchal solutions; others count of flexibility and decentralised communities. Some other organisms don't have a central organ or brain. However they can sense their environment better than animals by reliably assessing situations, reacting to external stimuli and communicating with one another. Simple processes transform into complex ones and all without a brain.

Lichens for example are known to be the world's slowest telegram. They memorise survival strategies for certain events and then pass on that information to others. This means they can be used as bioindicators for weather, light and air pollution. Moreover, lichens are a fascinating invention of evolution for more reasons than just passing on information. Next to their amazing aesthetic, they incorporate much more poetry. Lichens are a natural polygamy—a threesome of fungi, bacteria/algae and yeast—with better in-and external communication than most political parties as they're trustworthy, reliable and connected to the outside world.

These ecosystems cover six percent of the earth's surface while resisting not only heat and cold, but toxicity and time. The strategies these other organisms use to organise their functionalities are efficient ways for a sustainable and democratic life. They use very little energy, survive under extreme conditions, learn from experience and find thousands of solutions for problems that are different from the ones we experience. Such problems like material scarcity, cooperation (or lack thereof), ageing, autonomic energy supply, compromises and adaption. The modular structure, resistance and flexibility of these other intelligences must be incorporated into the modern age.

Isn't this enough to consider them and other species as a source of inspiration.

What can we learn from them?
Where will they guide us?

A cold and bluish evening in Eindhoven
Full of noise and smog
Where strange and intelligent creatures
Spring from concrete and trees
Leading us the way to resource our bodies
	with fresh and pure air

344°N
51°26'24"N
5° 28'32 '' E

Let's follow them!

Grey lichens tell us to go straight
Then to turn back
Lost
Confused
The ones which fit perfectly the tree's bark
In the middle of a neighbourhood full
	of row-houses
Garnered our attention

Further north
The freezing weather left those organic
	intelligences fresh and dry

Lichens give less room for compass and
	digital devises
And guide us to a quiet place
Bright and yellow
They sleep so peacefully
Far away from the bustle of the city

(What seems as blank matter
has intelligent processes.
mountains, oceans, clouds
could there be something?)

The Parable

Josh Plough

Defined as a simple story used to illustrate a moral or spiritual lesson. That's how we can end this book. A lot has happened since the essays were commissioned and the book started to take shape: the crackdown in Hong Kong, the poisoning of political dissidents, the pandemic, the increased surveillance of employees in their homes...the list goes on. But so too do the stories.

Often publications are the end of action, with intentions cast in ink. But stories have the abilities to keep on travelling as their spoken. So after reading this book, think about the links between the EU and China's authoritarian and genocidal regime: speak it out loud. This way we are forced to think about some things that we'd rather not. The invisibility of these links is built into this system of oppression and behaviour modification.

While the Netherlands and China are seen as being at different ends of the spectrum when it comes to surveillance, the Triangulum Project partnership somewhat discredits that assumption.[1] What makes the link between Eindhoven and Tianjin so important is that it's the perfect example to show to those who still believe in the amoral utility of technology. The very aim of having Tianjin be part of the project is because it "presents significant opportunities for the industrial and private sector partners involved...to access and exploit the Chinese smart city market".[2] So theoretically, what is tested on the people of Eindhoven without popular knowledge or consent could be used by the Chinese surveillance state to oppress and suppress its citizens.

So yes, we're lucky that cities like Eindhoven are pushing for strict local data laws, but what happens when the technologies honed on an unassuming and allegedly anonymised public crosses borders? For now this is all speculation. But it serves as an illustration for those who can't make the leap between technologies in European cities and the desire for total control. When Footnotes ran workshops addressing these issues we often had the "Oh but that would never happen here" reaction. This is something we cannot guarantee and the potential for misuse is implicit when there are direct links to the Chinese surveillance state.

We as citizens must show solidarity. If we cannot put a stop to these surveillance start ups—those intent on the quantification and commodification of life—then we must write new laws concerning the weaponisation of technology, and the many definitions that can take. We must assume a responsibility for each other, because companies have no loyalties but to the market: it's just business after all.

We mustn't let these stories become epitaphs. So go and join a cause, telling them that a story brought you there.

1
https://smartcities-infosystem.eu/
sites-projects/projects/triangulum

2
https://web.archive.org/web/20200815082420/
https://www.triangulum-project.eu/?page_
id=2355

Biographies

Sjamme van de Voort has written his PhD dissertation at the University of Nottingham in which he investigates the relationship between frames of cultural memory and subjective imaginaries of Cubans in Miami-Dade County, USA. This allowed him to elaborate a methodology for investigations of memories in migration and ideologies of exile. Other projects include research on the use of the internet in Cuba and freedom of speech. Together with Moniek Driesse, Sjamme forms the transdisciplinary research collective The Imaginary Agency, through which they investigate urban imaginaries and mnemonic dynamics.

Bas Grutjes has been an anarchist all his life, with mixed results in different capacities: activist, toilet attendant, teacher, bouncer, web designer, organiser of punk concerts, founder of a small library, collector of meaning. Since 2015 he writes about austerity, the extreme right, mainstream racism, refugee policies, surveillance capitalism, and other forms of dehumanisation. He develops fantasy worlds for games & occasionally writes stories. He wishes the revolution would hurry up a bit. He'd like to write children's books & compose new musical worlds, but there's simply no time. You can find his blog on grutjes.nl. Also, he keeps the universe in an old jam jar in the cupboard under his stairs. Don't ask, don't tell.

Helen Milne is a designer/researcher born in Bristol, UK and currently based in the Netherlands. Her background is in Textile Design (specifically weaving) and holds a Masters degree in Contextual Design from Design Academy Eindhoven, 2020. Since the first publication of her article, she has been involved in a working group for Gemeente Eindhoven, finally signing off on a new covenant road-mapping the future of Student Housing for the next ten years. She is hopeful for better things to come.

Pete Ho Ching Fung is a designer whose situated practice explores the meanings constructed through our individual and collective lived experiences. His fluid approach moves between words and images, interventions and collaborations, theoretical and artistic research. Grounded in decoloniality theories, his work seeks to decentralise the single stories within our everyday lives - the known knowledge(s), social relations, designed environments and technologies. He runs *Design for the Time Being*, an editorial platform investigating the realities proposed by Design and designing.

Josh Plough is writer and curator currently based in Warsaw where he has founded the cultural NGO *Ziemniaki i.* The aim of which is to research the contemporary relevance of myth and folklore by placing them in the constellation of politics, digital technologies and creativity. He's also working out how art and design research can be embedded into local and governmental structures.

Wibke Bramsfeld (she/her) is an independent German graphic designer based in Rotterdam. With her design practice Studio Bramesfeld she focuses mainly on book design and visual communication, usually in the broad field of the cultural sector. Her approach is to not only create a purely beautiful design but to convey the individual content by taking graphic, typography, colour and materials into consideration. Always with an eagerness to expand, learn and grow.

Kai Landolt is passionate about exploring and testing how human needs are shaped by the constant fluctuation of technologies, normalities and public opinion. His underlying interest in physical objects has been transcended by the digital era. As someone with a product design background, he's intrigued by our relationship between our computerised and physical world. Currently he is a UI/UX freelancer and researcher at Fonty's Journalism and Responsible Innovation research group.

Jakob Schleenvoigt is an industrial designer by training who is currently stumbling around in the world of communication design and art trying to find ways to change the world without emitting too much CO2. He likes to dissect human-made structures into their assumptions, has a love-hate-relationship towards things that make sense and is currently in the process of overcoming an ideology called modernism. In March 2021 his homebase was in Amsterdam.

Leon Barre, born in Hamburg, Germany, is a student of the Food Non Food department at Design Academy Eindhoven. As a child he always wanted to study medicine: to heal and support people, to make them feel better. But when realising the twisted economics of the health system he ran off. This original urge manifested itself in an interest for food as an expression of care for people and the environment. Leon also creates worlds for people to escape and dream in. To retreat back to their ‚inner child‘, to the valuable unbiased intermediary spaces of play & dialogue in which we learn and grow so much.

Wendy Owusu, Born in 1994, lives and works between Paris and Eindhoven. She is currently completing her Bachelor degree at the Design Academy Eindhoven, the Netherlands. With a multidisciplinary practice that works across video, textile, publishing and installation, she focuses on sociology, mapping and afrodescendant cultures.

Lotte Houwing is a policy advisor and researcher at Bits of Freedom. She focuses mainly on the relationship between the State and the citizen and the balance of power that goes with it. For example, she works on a case focused on the secret services and the investigative powers of the police. Lotte is committed to protecting citizens against the misuse of power.

Colophon

**Eindhoven Footnotes:
Tales from a Technocratic City**

Onomatopee 161

ISBN:
978-94-93148-08-6

Edited by:
Josh Plough

Contributors:
Sjamme van de Voort,
Bas Grutjes,
Josh Plough,
Helen Milne,
Pete Ho Ching Fung,
Kai Landolt,
Lotte Houwing,
Jakob Schleenvoigt,
Leon Barre,
Wendy Owusu.

Designed by:
Wibke Bramsfeld

Printing:

Paper:

Typeface:
Authentic Sans

This project and publication were
made possible thanks to the
generous support of:

cultuur
eindhoven

SUPPORTED BY

stimuleringsfonds
creatieve industrie

Provincie Noord-Brabant

Published by:
Onomatopee Projects
Publisher and public gallery
www.onomatopee.net

People, Institutions and
Movements that Connected
Through Footnotes:

Aaron Garlick
Agnieszka Piksa
Alorah Harman
Alejandro Cerón
April Xie
Arthur Van De Poll
Barbora Stredova
Bas Grutjes
becoming.network
Ben van de Broek
Callum Dean
Clodaegh Read
Colin Keays
Christo Weijs
Cristina Cochior
Dario Sposini
Design Academy Eindhoven
DIT is Transitie in Eindhoven
Dirk Visscher
Dominik Stanislawski
Dr. Sergio M. Figueiredo
Eindhoven Heritage House
Eindhoven Student Housing
Protest
Els Vervloesem
Eva de Bruijn
Frederik Pesch
Freja Bäckman
Freek Lomme
Fundacja IMAGO MUNDI
Giulio Squillacciotti
Giuseppe Licari
Helen Milne
Henryk Makarewicz

Immony Men
Jacob Voorthuis
Jacqueline Schoemaker
Jakob Schleenvogt
Jaro Varga
Jip Sanders
Jim Brady
Joana Chicau
Justin Agyin
Kai Landolt
Kees Kluskens
Kris Dittel
Krzysztof Maniak
Lennart Arpots
Leon Huets
Leon Barre
Liza Willemsen
Louise Gholam
Lotte Houwing
Łukasz Błażejewski [Prince
Negatif]
Łukasz Trzciński
Łukasz Skąpski
Marle Rime
Michel op den Camp
Miodrag Kuč
Moniek Drisse
Noam Youngrak Son
Noud Sleumer
Paolo Patelli
Patricio Davila
Pernilla Ellens
Pete Ho Ching Fung
Pio Bujak
Prof. dr. ir. Sonia Heemstra de
Groot
Radicalzz
RaRaRadio

Richard Ponjee
Robin Weidner
Ruden van de Ven
Rutger Schimmel
Siem Nozza
Sjamme van de Voort
Stanisław Ruksza
Stephanie van den Hurk
Tea Ferrari
The Imaginary Agency
Tinus Kanters
Tomáš Moravec
TU / Eindhoven
Vladimir Palibrk
Wendy Owusu
Wibke Bramesfeld
Wiktor Pental

Special Thanks to:
Timothy Donaldson for granting us permission to use Donald-sansCODE in its beta form for use in our zines. This humanist monospaced typeface represents an alternative relationship towards technology in the context of the 'smart' city. His fonts are available through <www.timothydonaldson.org>.

Yorit Kluitman for supplying additional graphic resources and elements of the visual identity for the research space and promotional material.

Eindhoven Picture Archives for the support and warm welcome each time we came to look through their collections. And also to the Erfgoedhuis Eindhoven (Heritage House) for their knowledge, patience and generosity.

Callum Dean for his design work for the zines, constant involvement and support. Eindhoven Footnotes would not have been possible without you!

The Allegories Lichelligence, Tracing Identities and Materialising Data were the results of a collaboration between Eindhoven Footnotes and the Design

Academy Eindhoven. Paolo Patelli, associate lector of the Lectorate Places and Traces, worked together with the students to unpack the smart city. A big thank you to him and all the students who contributed work and ideas.

And finally to everyone who turned up to the meetings and supported Footnotes with their time and labour. It was a struggle to reach out to the public. But we're so thankful to the people who engaged with the project and its processes.

A Final Note:
As has been noted by one of authors in the book, the process to get this in your hands has been slower than usual and fraught with missteps. As the editor I would like to apologise again for the drawn out processes and excess stress this has caused. I can't thank all the contributors enough for all their work and dedication to producing a book that dulls the lustre of our radiant machines.